MW01042236

Thank you for your service!
I hope you had a great flight
and enjoy my book.

Larry Reedy

Batesville Shooter
and Friends

Batesville Shooter *and* Friends

Gun Reviews, Shooting Accessories, and Gun-Related Advice

Larry Reidy

ORANGE *frazer* PRESS
Wilmington, Ohio

ISBN 978-1949248-432
Copyright ©2021 Larry Reidy
All Rights Reserved

No part of this publication may be reproduced in any material form (including photocopying or storing in any medium by electronic means and whether or not transiently or incidentally to some other use of this publication) without the written permission of the copyright holder except in accordance with the provisions of Title 17 of the United States Code.

The images, views, and opinions in this book belong to the author and copyright holder and do not represent the images, views, and opinions of Orange Frazer Press, Inc. The mere appearance in this publication does not contribute to endorsement by Orange Frazer Press, Inc.. Orange Frazer Press, Inc. hereby disclaims any and all liability to any party for any direct, indirect, implied, punitive, special, incidental, or other consequential damages arising directly or indirectly from any use of any information provided in this book.

Library of Congress Control Number:
2021908004

Printed in the United States of America

First Printing

Dedication

I dedicate this book to responsible gun owners
worldwide, law enforcement, the military,
and future gun owners.

Acknowledgments

I appreciate my friends for their reviews and input. I thank my wife, Nancy, for her support, my family, friends, and the people who read and gave me great reviews on my first book, *My Quest for Life, Liberty, and the Pursuit of Happiness, from 1939–2019*. I want to thank Sandy Zeigler, a Batesville photographer, who captured the fire blast from my M1A Socom for the cover. She is also responsible for the photo on the back of the book. Her website is studioten86photography.com.

Table of Contents

Author's Note

God Bless America. I pray that the politicians do not infringe on our right to bear arms.

I have always tried to make economic decisions in business that made sense. My book has approximately 250 photos and, to save quite a bit of money, the smart move was to have a Chinese printing company do the printing and binding. My principles took over my decision making. My book was printed in our great country, and I will continue to be guided by my principles, not by financial gain.

Introduction

My book is based on my website, batesvilleshooter. com. My site was published on October 28, 2016, and has over 500,000 visitors and 22,000 subscribers. I own 115 guns and have a 200 yard rifle range and a pistol range. If I purchased any more weapons, I think my wife would try to commit me to a mental institution.

I am not an expert on firearms, so as you read my reviews, remember that these are just my opinions. I thank my friends who took the time to write a review on their guns.

Batesville Shooter
and **Friends**

I
Revolvers

Smith & Wesson
K22 Masterpiece

Smith & Wesson K22 Masterpiece. I purchased this revolver in 1962. I changed the grips and still have the originals: fun and cheap shooting. Phenomenal quality. I posted a YouTube video that is informative and entertaining on my website. I want to revisit this post of my K22 Masterpiece because this pistol is impressive. I purchased this pistol fifty-seven years ago, and it is still accurate, looks like it's brand new, and performs flawlessly. The reason that I am posting this revolver first is it brings back great memories. While I was in the Army serving in the Panama Canal Zone I purchased my first K22 at the Post PX for $29.00 or $39.00. It was a great pistol, and I sold it to a friend of mine when I left the Canal Zone for the states to receive my honorable discharge. The K22 Masterpiece is my first purchase of any weapon. I try to fire at least fifty rounds once a year with this great revolver! I highly recommend YouTube for videos for the old and new Smith & Wesson 22 revolvers.

Review: November 11, 2019

Ruger Super Redhawk 44 Magnum

The Ruger Super Redhawk 44 Magnum is a hand cannon. I love shooting this revolver! It has quite a bit of recoil, and it's very accurate. The quality of the weapon is superb, and the stopping power is phenomenal. A few years ago, my daughter Julie invited two guest teachers from Spain to visit Nancy and me in Batesville. Spain does not allow gun ownership, so they were amazed at my gun collection. I gave them a safety class and started their shooting experience with a 22LR. We moved up to a 9mm. My grandson, David, was also shooting. I asked the teachers and David if they would like to shoot a 44 Magnum, and they had a Dirty Harry smile on their face and enthusiastically said yes. I demonstrated firing the beast before they each fired five rounds. The teachers didn't hit the target, and David placed four rounds on cardboard, not the target. He was proud that he was somewhat near his ultimate destination. His ego shattered when I pointed out that four of his rounds hit the concrete and ricocheted onto the cardboard.

There are great videos on YouTube featuring the Super Redhawk and the Super Redhawk Alaska.

Review: October 28, 2016

Smith & Wesson 357 Combat Magnum Model 19

I purchased my Smith & Wesson 357 Magnum Combat Magnum in 1966. The S&W is a great revolver! I chose this model over Colt Python because the double action of the Smith, in my opinion, was a lot smoother. I believe I paid between $400.00 and $500.00, which was about the Python price. Colt discontinued their model before S&W discontinued the Model 19 Combat Magnum so on the used market, the Python is selling for $1,800.00–$4,000.00. S&W has reintroduced Model 19, and if you are looking for an excellent revolver, I highly recommend Model 19. There are unique videos on YouTube, and I highly recommend Hickok45 and Team Sooch. Hickok45 also has a great video on a Colt Python. I had a couple of exciting experiences with my Combat Magnum that I will share.

Thirty-six years ago, my wife, Nancy, woke me out of a sound sleep at 2:00 A.M. and told me that someone pulled in our driveway and turned their lights out. I did what any reasonable person would do. I put on a pair of pants, walked out the back door, sneaked around the car to the driver's door, and placed the barrel of my 357 Magnum against his head. I asked him if he was lost. He replied, "Jesus Christ, Mr. Reidy, don't shoot; it's me, David." David is a friend of my son, Larry, and I told David that I didn't think that it was a good idea for him to stop at our home at 2:00 A.M. with his lights out. We never had another late-night intruder!

I was interviewing a young man for a sales position for my company in the mid-1970s when my secretary interrupted me because Nancy was on the phone and needed to speak to me. She told me that the children and our miniature Schnauzer, Sniffles, had a groundhog cornered, and she needed some advice to handle the situation. I said, "Get the 357 Magnum and shoot the son-of-a-bitch." When I finished the conversation, the gentleman I interviewed told me that he did not want to work for me and was almost running towards the door. Go figure! *Review: September 10, 2018*

Uberti
Bird's Head

My brother Ron will be ninety-two in December and due to some recent health problems, he decided to give some of his guns to relatives. I received a Uberti Bird's Head chambered in 357 Magnum. Uberti manufactures old west replica models, and the quality is excellent. Uberti was purchased by the Beretta group several years ago, and their upgraded manufacturing process is unique. My Bird's Head has a three-and-a-half-inch barrel and is an excellent twenty to twenty-five feet revolver. Cimarron Arms also sells the old West replicas and Uberti manufactures most of their product. If you like single-action revolvers and want to own models that are a part of our country's history, Uberti or Cimarron have excellent guns. The Uberti has minimal recoil and is fun to shoot. *Review: August 14, 2018*

Update: Brother Ron died in May of 2020 at the age of niney-three, brother Bill died in February 2012 at the age of eighty, so I am the "Last of the Mohicans."

Smith & Wesson Governor with Crimson Trace Laser Grips

I have posted reviews on all of my guns, I think, a couple of weapons that I borrowed from Guns and Tackle in Greensburg, Indiana, and a few welcome reviews from friends. I ask people regularly to review some of their guns, and I get very little response. I will have to borrow some guns or buy some and risk my wife trying to commit me to a funny farm or get some reviews from people who enjoy the website. In the meantime, I will list some guns that I hope will stay in the family when it is time for me to go to the Heavenly Shooting Range. I will not try to dictate to my children from the grave, but anyone who has a gun collection is probably thinking the same way as me. My list will not be in any specific order, but my reasoning will be quality, accuracy, sentimental, and fun to shoot. I hope you enjoy this and maybe make your list for your heirs. The Governor is unique and chambered in 45ACP, 45 Colt, and 410 shotgun shells. Excellent quality, accurate, great for concealed carry and home protection. This revolver is fun to shoot. I reviewed The Governor on March 8, 2017. Recently, while shooting this excellent revolver, I thought this is a phenomenal weapon. I forgot to mention the Crimson Trace Laser grips. They are useless in the sun but are terrific at night. Great videos on YouTube! *Review Update: March 26, 2018*

Ruger Single Six Convertible 22LR/ 22 Magnum

I have a Ruger Single Six Convertible purchased forty-five to forty-seven years ago, and it still looks new. The Ruger is an excellent revolver for the first time or experienced shooter. It has adjustable front and rear sights and is very accurate with either the 22LR or 22 Magnum. The finish and the walnut grips are of excellent quality. The more recent single six models manufactured in the early seventies have a safety block so you can load six rounds without a possible discharge. This model by Ruger has been in continuous production since 1953, with a few changes along the way. Before you buy a new Single-Six Convertible for around $600.00, read my upcoming review on the Heritage Rough Rider. Team Sooch and other considerations are available on YouTube.

Review: November 3, 2017

Ruger LCR 22LR and LCR 22 Magnum

The Ruger LCR 22LR and 22 Magnum are excellent revolvers for anyone who has a problem with recoil. Most people think that 9mm, 40, or 45 calibers are what you need for home protection. I disagree because when a person gets intimated by the recoil and cannot hit the target, you would be better off shooting the person in a self-defense situation with a small-caliber round than missing with a more powerful cartridge. Check out YouTube videos. *Review: September 3, 2017*

Heritage Rough Rider Convertible 22LR/ 22 Magnum

The Heritage Rough Rider is an inexpensive, quality revolver available for purchase for $200.00 to $250.00. I have fired hundreds of rounds through mine and have never had any problems. It has fixed sights like the original Colt Single Action Army and the original Ruger Single Six. The sights are not the most accurate, but you can always use Kentucky windage. Example: If you shoot high left, lower your sightline, and move it to the right. I like my Ruger Single Six, but it is not worth three times the Rough Rider price. Hickok 45 has an excellent video on YouTube.

Review: November 9, 2017

Ruger LCR 357 Magnum

The Ruger LCR 357 is an excellent gun for a glove compartment in your automobile and possibly a concealed carry. I am not comfortable carrying a five-shot revolver. The 357 Magnum is a perfect round with incredible stopping power, but it is gratifying to shoot in a full-size gun, not a small snub nose with considerable recoil. I fired five shots rapid fire at thirty feet using the point and shoot method and had excellent results. Several YouTube videos are informative and entertaining. One of the videos highlights the difference in the recoil of the 357 versus the 38 Special. *Review: August 22, 2017*

Ruger Vaquero
357 Magnum

The Ruger Vaquero is a classic single-action revolver that is quite elegant and fun to shoot. My Ruger is chambered in 357 Magnum or 38 Special. The Vaquero is strictly a range gun, and in my opinion, no single-action revolver is adequate for home defense. The Ruger is a big revolver, and the recoil is very manageable because of the size. The old-fashioned sights are not very good when trying to hit a bullseye on a paper target, but you will be able to hit steel targets from a reasonable distance. I like this revolver and highly recommend it to anyone who wants to shoot just for the fun of it. The Vaquero is a modern-day weapon that links us to the great history of the West's early days.

Review: December 27, 2016

Ruger Single Action Bisley Revolver 45ACP/ 45 Colt

The Ruger Bisley convertible revolver allows you to fire two different caliber cartridges, the 45ACP and the 45 Long Colt. I prefer shooting 45ACP because of the price difference. This revolver is like having a gun from the old West. It is not for home protection or concealed carry. There is a great post describing the Bisley on Wikipedia. It is a different grip that is supposed to limit recoil. I do not know if that is true since this is the only revolver that I own chambered in 45ACP/ Long Colt. The Bisley also has a very nice engraved cylinder in the 45 Long Colt. The Bisley is an excellent recreational revolver! I could not find any great videos on YouTube for this model.

The Ruger Bisley, manufactured by Sturm Ruger & Company, is a five- or six-shot, single-action revolver. It comes in a variety of different finishes, calibers, and barrel lengths. The gun takes its name from a grip frame designed by Colt's Manufacturing Company that was popular at Bisley's shooting matches.

Review: January 18, 2017

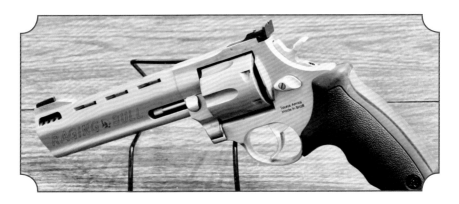

Taurus
Raging Bull

I recently purchased a Taurus Raging Bull Chambered in 44 Magnum. I like the price, trigger, balance, and quality. I don't like the black front sight, and the grip feels good until you shoot about twenty-five rounds. I was shooting single action into the sun at thirty-five feet. I had to adjust the rear sight and put a dab of white

Ruger

Taurus

paint on the front sight. I alternated every six rounds with my Ruger Super Redhawk. The Ruger performed flawlessly at thirty-five feet. I fired both firearms at 1-2 second intervals. I posted targets, and my final two shots from the Ruger were at thirty-five yards hitting the target high left. *Review: August 16, 2020*

Colt Python
357 Magnum

In the late sixties, I decided to buy a 357 Magnum revolver. My choices were a Smith & Wesson Combat Magnum or a Colt Python. I opted for the Combat Magnum. On September 30, 2020, I purchased a Colt Python at the Indiana Gun Club. In my opinion, the latest Python is an improvement over the original. I love the look, quality, trigger, and value. I am glad that I purchased my Combat Magnum because I am more accurate with the S&W, and it just feels better in my hand. *Review: October 4, 2020*

Update: After firing two-hundred rounds through my new Python, my accuracy has improved, and the trigger pull, double and single action, is one of the best. January 6, 2021

Smith & Wesson
44 Magnum

Today was a perfect day for my favorite hobby, shooting. One of the revolvers that I shot is a Smith & Wesson model 629-8 44 Magnum from the Performance Center. What a magnificent handgun! I was shooting rapid-fire from thirty-five feet. The last three shots were from twenty-five yards going for a head shot. The top left hole on the target had two shots in the same hole. Pure luck! I have two revolvers from the S&W Performance Center, and it's hard to believe how accurate they are right out of the box. *Review: October 4, 2020*

Smith & Wesson
Thunder Ranch 45ACP

The Thunder Ranch is another excellent revolver from the S&W Performance Center. I was pleasantly surprised by the accuracy and little recoil from a short barrel revolver. The quality, trigger, sights, and grips are excellent. The Thunder Ranch is a must if you are buying a 45ACP revolver. I was shooting rapid-fire at thirty-five feet at the target above. *Review: October 4, 2020*

Smith & Wesson
22 Magnum

I recently purchased a Smith & Wesson 22 Magnum from the S&W classic series. It looks and feels like my K22 Masterpiece that I purchased fifty-eight years ago. The Smith revolvers have excellent triggers, sights, and finish. My Magnum is very accurate and fun to shoot. Fortunately, I have about seven hundred rounds of 22 Magnum cartridges. Ammunition is hard to get and extremely expensive due to the surge of people buying firearms and stocking up on ammo. Depending on the election outcome in two days, ammo will be more available or almost impossible to buy at a reasonable price. *Review: November 1, 2020*

II
Pistols

CZ 75
Compact

I wanted to update my review for this excellent pistol. I recently fired about one hundred rounds, and the trigger seems to get better every time I shoot the CZ. I highly recommend the CZ for home protection.

Update: June 14, 2020

The CZ 75 is an excellent 9mm semi-automatic pistol. The 9mm handgun field has so many great choices for quality pistols that it is challenging to have a favorite. There are several versions of the CZ 75 compact, and the model that I have is all steel. In my opinion, it is too big and bulky for concealed carry. This pistol is at home on the range. It fits my hand like a glove, is very accurate, and has a mild recoil. This high-quality pistol sells for $550.00 if you can find one. The CZ 75 has low profit margins for dealers, so don't expect discounts. *Review: October 15, 2019*

Colt 1911 Commander

I reviewed my son Ted's Colt 1911 Commander and his Beretta Nano. I would not recommend the Nano because the trigger is awful. I have a few Berettas that I like, but the Nano isn't on my list to own or ever shoot again. There are quite a few sub-compacts that are excellent.

Ted's Commander's design is about twenty-five years old. It has an excellent trigger and is well balanced, but the sights are just like the Army's 1911s. I recommended that my son change the sights or put a white paint dab on the front sight. There are some great 1911s available, and I have reviewed several of my 1911s. *Review: October 3, 2019*

Smith & Wesson
380 Shield EZ

The S&W 380 Shield EZ is an excellent pistol for a beginner, someone who has arthritis, a person who wants less recoil than a 9mm, an older adult, or someone who doesn't have the strength to rack the slide on other semi-automatics. The EZ is light and very accurate at twenty–thirty feet. The magazines hold eight rounds, and I had four failures to eject while shooting the first two magazines. The following 150 rounds had no problems. Once in a while, when breaking in a pistol, the magazines are stiff. I put this pistol through a test for defensive purposes, not target shooting. I was shooting from thirty feet while moving, in a crouch position, one-handed, two-handed, left-handed, and all were rapid-fire with two or three bursts. There are excellent videos on YouTube for the 380EZ, and I highly recommend this pistol. I added a Crimson Trace Laser sight to the gun. *Review: May 18, 2019*

Ruger
Mark 4 Hunter

I have a previous review posted on batesvilleshooter. com about the Mark 4 Hunter, but this is compared to the other 22LR pistols that I own. The reviews are strictly my opinion and, before purchasing any gun, I would read and watch reviews on YouTube. The Ruger Mark 4 is an excellent pistol, and for my test, I was shooting at twenty, thirty, and forty feet, and most of my shooting was rapid-fire. Below is my score chart:

Sights	10	Accuracy	8	Magazines	10
Trigger	8	Ease of Cleaning	10	Brand Confidence	10
Fit and Finish	10	Reliability	10	Price	10
Grips	10	Fun to Shoot	10		
				Total Score	106

Review: April 18, 2019. Update: January 12, 2021. I like to shoot 22LR handguns and rifles. The ammo is inexpensive, and great 22LR firearms are available. The Hunter is a bit pricey compared to some of the other manufacturers' 22LR guns, but, in my opinion, it's a great value based on the quality and the fun factor. There is an excellent video by Hickok45 on YouTube.

Browning Buck Mark

Today was a great day to shoot my Browning Buck Mark! The Buck Mark is an excellent 22LR, and I will use the same criteria for my review that I used on the Ruger 22/45 Lite. The ammo used was CCI Mini-Mag, 36 grain, 1260 feet per second that are faster than the speed of sound. Below is my score chart:

Sights	9	Accuracy	8	Magazines	10
Trigger	9	Ease of Cleaning	8*	Brand Confidence	10
Fit and Finish	8	Reliability	10	Price	9
Grips	9	Fun to Shoot	10		
				Total Score	100

The reason for the asterisk at the rating for ease of cleaning is Browning does not recommend field stripping the Buck Mark. If they recommended field stripping, I would have given it a 6.

Review: March 27, 2019

Update: In October 2020, I purchased another Buck Mark at Indiana Gun Club. I couldn't resist buying it because of the excellent price. There is something about shooting the Browning pistols; the perfect balance, outstanding trigger, and fit and finish are extraordinary.

Ruger
22/45 Lite

I finally had a beautiful day to shoot my Ruger 22/45 Lite. It's an excellent pistol in a very crowded field of great 22LR pistols and revolvers. I should have purchased a more expensive optic. The Monstrom red/green dot optic was $49.00 and, for the money, is okay. I have the same optic on a Smith & Wesson Victory. I have several 22LR pistols that I am going to compare against the 22/45 Lite. The comparison will be my opinion, and I know it certainly is not meant to be the right one for everyone. I will use only CCI ammo while making comparisons. I never have misfires with CCI ammo, but some other brands are not as reliable with various pistols. I will grade each handgun on a ten-point system in eleven categories starting today with the 22/45 Lite. Below is my score chart:

Sights	8	Accuracy	8	Magazines	10
Trigger	7	Ease of Cleaning	10	Brand Confidence	10
Fit and Finish	8	Reliability	9	Price	8
Grips	8	Fun to Shoot	10		
				Total Score	96

The previous test was the Browning Buck Mark.

Review: March 14, 2019

Double Tap Defense 9mm Derringer

I am reposting this for anyone who might be thinking about purchasing a small derringer. I won a Double Tap 9mm derringer from an FOP raffle a few years ago. My first thoughts were it has an excellent design, it's a two-shot over and under pistol about the size of a deck of cards, it has storage for two rounds in the grip, weighs about thirteen ounces, and drops in a pocket. My second thoughts were, I bet the recoil is awful, and who would want a concealed carry pistol with just two rounds. To evaluate my FOP winner, I had to shoot this beast. The recoil was worse than I imagined. It hurt so bad that if I was in a defensive situation and fired two rounds and had to reload to fire two more rounds, I would probably wonder if I might feel better getting shot than returning fire. I will never fire this pistol again, and I would never sell it because I wouldn't wish this derringer on my worst enemy. A YouTube video is worth watching to see the reaction after shooting the Double Tap at a range.

Review: September 24, 2018

Wilson Combat
CQB 1911

My Wilson Combat CQB (Close Quarters Combat) 1911 is my favorite handgun. The quality is phenomenal, the accuracy is excellent and the trigger and sights are the best for shooting any 1911. The CQB MSRP starts at about $2,800.00. That is a lot of money for one pistol. If you want a top-notch 1911 but you do not want to spend the money, I have a recommendation. Buy an inexpensive 1911 such as a Remington R1, and send it to Wilson Combat for upgrades. I spent $650.00 for my Remington, paid $800.00 for Wilson upgrades, and cannot tell any difference when shooting them. *Review: July 6, 2018*

Beretta 92FS customized by Wilson Combat & Wilson Brigadier

I have two more recommended keepers for my children. I purchased a Beretta 92FS around 1985, and I always enjoyed shooting it. I think it was around four years ago when I sent it to Wilson Combat for some custom work. I believe that I paid $300.00–$500.00 for the 92FS when I purchased it, and I think I spent around $750.00 for the custom work. It was worth the money spent. Several months later, Wilson and Beretta joined to produce the Brigadier, which is a 92FS customized. I cannot tell the difference while shooting these excellent pistols. Sights, slide, grips, and triggers are outstanding. The Brigadier sells for around $1,200.00. Excellent videos are available on YouTube.

Review: April 2, 2018

Sig Sauer
P220 45ACP

Sig manufactures great pistols and rifles, and they are a little pricey. The P220 was introduced in 1976 and is still a popular choice. I believe that I purchased mine about five years ago. Through the years, Sig has made some changes. My P220 is a single-stack magazine that holds seven rounds in the magazine plus one in the chamber. The P220s today have eight-round magazines. The sights are better than average and the trigger is decent but not great. It has an excellent grip and good accuracy. I have never had a malfunction of any kind with any of my Sigs. The P220, in my opinion, is too big for concealed carry, and I would rather have a higher capacity magazine for home protection. The

P220 has excellent stopping power, and is fun to shoot, but, in my opinion, there are too many other options in the marketplace. There is a nice five-year-old video by Hickok45 on YouTube that I think is informative and entertaining. *Review: September 15, 2017*

Ruger
SR 9

The Ruger SR 9 might be the best buy for home protection. It is chambered in 9mm, has excellent sights, excellent capacity (17+1), nice balance, decent trigger and reset, very reliable, and outstanding warranty service. The main reason for me qualifying this as a possible best buy for home protection is the price. Retail is $569.00, but I have seen prices from $429.00 to $489.00. I have never had a misfire, and I probably fired a thousand rounds through the SR 9. There are so many good choices in the 9mm category, but your home protection piece is usually in a quick-access safe in your bedroom and not fired too often. Excellent YouTube videos on the SR 9 by Hickok45 and Team Sooch! *Review: March 6, 2018*

Colt 1911 Gold Cup National Match

The Gold Cup Match is one of my favorite 1911s and the first one that I purchased. I was a military policeman in the Army, and 1911 was my carry piece. Usually, by the 15th of each month, I was broke, so I spent quite a bit of time at the shooting range with my Army issued 1911. One day, I was shooting with a buddy of mine and I told him that I always qualified sharpshooter but just wasn't good enough to qualify expert. He was on the Canal Zone Army pistol team and he allowed me to shoot his gold cup match pistol. It was a night and day difference. I said I could qualify expert with this Colt Gold Cup Match pistol so how can I get the Army to issue one to me. He said it's effortless. Try out for the pistol team and qualify expert with your Army issue 1911. He was a smart ass. I purchased my Gold Cup in 1985, and I am sure the more recent models have some changes. I don't know how they could improve this pistol. It has excellent balance and sights, and the trigger reset is spectacular. There are excellent videos from YouTube on some of the newer Colt Gold Cup Match because I couldn't find any manufactured in the mid-eighties. *Review: February 20, 2018*

Walther
PPS .40

The Walther PPS chambered in .40 caliber is an excellent concealed carry pistol in a crowded segment. The pros are size, grip, reliability, cost, and accuracy. In my opinion, the cons are the trigger, .40 caliber, and low capacity single stack magazine (7/8 rounds). A 9mm is a better choice for concealed carry, and Walther must think it is a better option because their newer model

PPS M2 is chambered in 9mm. The older PPS is chambered in 9mm or .40 caliber. There are several YouTube videos on this pistol. *Review: February 20, 2018*

Glock G22
Gen 4

The Glock G22 is chambered in .40 caliber. It is one of the most popular pistols used by police agencies in the United States. The reasons for the 60 to 70% popularity by law enforcement are (1) Thirteen round standard magazines versus ten round magazines for 45ACP. (2) Less recoil than a 45ACP round. (3) More stopping power than a 9mm with a minor increase in recoil. I purchased my Glock 22 when ammo was costly and hard to get. Since ammo is plentiful, the 40 is very close to the 45ACP in price, and the 9mm ammo is a bargain. The .40 caliber has been in existence since 1990. There are two videos on YouTube by Hickok45.

Review: December 27, 2017

Smith & Wesson
Victory 22LR Kryptek

I reviewed the Victory on December 27, 2017. The reason for another review is this one has a Monstrum red dot/ green dot optic that was very inexpensive ($30.00). Kryptek is just the camouflage version of the Victory. The Victory is a great target pistol with the original sights or using an optic. The most significant advantage for me using an optic is the quicker acquisition of a target. Smith & Wesson manufacture a great inexpensive target pistol and it is easy to clean.

Walther
PPK/S 22LR

The Walther PPK/S chambered in 22LR is a high-quality pistol manufactured in Germany. The PPK/S is fun to shoot, very accurate, and inexpensive. I believe you can purchase the PPK/S for around $350.00. The Walther P22 is the most popular 22LR pistol in the world. I reviewed that pistol on February 11, 2017. The P22 is less expensive than the PPK/S, but I prefer the PPK/S because it's a little heavier, easier to field strip, and it is a clone of the PPK chambered in 380. Use quality ammo with the PPK/S, and you will never have a problem. The 22LR ammo is very inexpensive today. Quality 22LR ammo can be purchased for $10.00 and under for 100 rounds. There are informative and entertaining videos on YouTube. *Review: November 15, 2017*

Smith & Wesson
Bodyguard 380

The Smith & Wesson Bodyguard 380 is a sub-compact concealed carry pistol that has some pros and cons. Pros: It's a pocket or purse pistol and has a laser sight. It's very inexpensive and has Smith & Wesson quality. The recoil is moderate. Cons: The accuracy is okay at twenty-one feet; beyond that distance, not very good. The pistol has a single purpose of concealed carry. The Bodyguard is not a home protection gun and I don't care for the trigger. The slide is stiff for some older people and anyone who has a strength problem with their hands. My opinions are probably in the minority. The Bodyguard has been a very popular concealed carry pistol. I carry a Ruger LCP in a pocket holster in the summer or going to some local destination in Batesville because I think the trigger is so much better, and in my opinion, that improves the accuracy. In my opinion, twenty-five feet is a reasonable range for this type of pistol. There are some videos from YouTube in case anyone is interested in a sub-compact pistol.

Review: October 28, 2017

Glock 30
45ACP

The Glock 30 is the sub-compact 45ACP. I am not a Glock hater, but I just do not do well when I am shooting Glocks and it's not something that I look forward to shooting at the range. Glocks are incredibly reliable, easy maintenance, and you will hit body mass. I am not a fan of Glocks, and my opinion is in the minority. Most of the people that I know love Glocks. I am thinking about sending one to Wilson Combat for some customization and maybe I will be more effective and enjoy shooting them. I don't like the 30 for home protection because of the ten-round magazine capacity, and, for concealed carry, I want something smaller. I fired twenty rounds of rapid-fire at thirty feet, and, like most Glocks, I tend to shoot left. Three ejections out of twenty rounds hit me in the middle of my forehead. There are several YouTube videos on the GEN 4 models, and I am sure that improvements were made over my five or six-year-old model.

Review: October 16, 2017

Springfield XDM 4.5/ chambered in 45ACP

Springfield manufactures quality guns, and the XDM is an excellent polymer pistol. I have owned this XDM for several years, and this is, in my opinion, one of the best buys in the marketplace. I am listing the reasons that I like this pistol. (1) The grip is the same as a 1911 and feels excellent. (2) The trigger is very good with a great reset, and it is something that I can fire two hundred rounds at the range and not have a sore finger. (3) High-capacity magazine, thirteen rounds plus one in the chamber. The sights are excellent. (4) Weight is thirty-one ounces empty. I have no negatives to list about the XDM. The Springfield is an ideal home protection pistol, and some would like it as a concealed carry pistol. I would use it as an open carry, but I prefer a smaller handgun for concealed carry.

Review: October 10, 2017

CZ Scorpion
EVO 3 S1 Pistol

I purchased this pistol because it's unique and is fun to shoot. This 9mm is a blowback semi-auto with a 7 1/2 inch barrel. The Scorpion is used by law enforcement agencies worldwide. The civilian version's difference is semi-auto versus law enforcement EVO is semi-auto and fully automatic. After firing twenty-five rounds, I ordered some replacement accessories. The pistol has ambidextrous safety. The right-side digs into the upper portion of your index finger. I will replace the right-side safety. I also ordered two thirty-round magazines and a speed loader. I am going to install an EOTECH Holographic sight that I have on my Wilson Combat AR-15. Most of my AR-15 shooting is 150 to 200 yards. I have scopes on all my other rifles because I shoot at some small steel. I'm thinking about purchasing a brace that will be an extension of the Scorpion, but I will not decide until I fire the pistol with the enhancements. *Review: November 1, 2020*

Update: I replaced the right-side safety, installed a Timney trigger and my EOTECH sight. The new trigger is a two ¼ pound pull versus a factory trigger ten pound pull. Wow, what a great gun! The Scorpion is addictive. The fun factor is off the charts. December 15, 2020

Sig Sauer P227
DA/SA 45ACP

The Sig P227 is another excellent handgun from Sig Sauer. The P227 is very similar to the Sig P220. In my opinion, it is a nice upgrade from the P220. The magazine holds ten rounds, and my P220 contains seven. I think the sights are better and I like the grip because it has more texture and it is a little wider. The trigger and accuracy on both guns are excellent. Sig manufactures excellent products at reasonable prices. There are a couple of entertaining and informative videos from YouTube. *Review: September 27, 2017*

HK
45

Heckler & Koch is a manufacturer of high-quality pistols and rifles. The only negative comment that I have heard about HK is the price. The quality is excellent, but their guns are pricey. I like my HK 45! The grip, the sights, and the finish are superb. I love the trigger, but the reset is different. It is a two-click reset and it takes a while to get accustomed to it. The magazine holds ten rounds plus one in the chamber. In my opinion the HK is too big for concealed carry but great for home protection and the range. I have several HK guns and I have never had a misfire or any problems. There are excellent videos on YouTube. *Review: September 21, 2017*

Glock
26

The baby Glock is a very nice sub-compact handgun. I have a first-generation 26, and the improvements for second, third and, fourth generations are, in my opinion, negligible. A significant number of people use the G26 as a concealed carry weapon. I am more comfortable with a full-size pistol or a compact pistol. I have my G26 in a safe on my nightstand. It has a fifteen extended round magazine and the stock ten-round magazine. I try to shoot this pistol every few months for practice using a point-and-shoot method. If there is a home invasion, no one will have the composure to use the sights, and it will probably be a situation without lights. I am not a fan of the factory sights on this pistol. *Review: August 16, 2017*

Sig Sauer
P226 Legion

The Sig P226 Legion is an excellent pistol that is enjoyable to shoot. Mike from Guns and Tackle in Greensburg, Indiana, offered to loan me the Legion to test and write a review. The trigger is the real star of the pistol! It is very smooth and has a reset comparable to the Wilson Combat Brigadier. The finish, grip, sights, slide, and accuracy are superb. The only drawback is the price. The MSRP is $1,413.00, but it can be purchased from the $1,200.00 to $1,300.00 range. I own several Sig pistols and they are very reliable. The YouTube videos that are available about the Legion were informative and entertaining. At Guns and Tackle, Mike gave me a tip to get a tighter grip while shooting rapid-fire and I can't wait until I try it. Mrgunsngear has an excellent video on YouTube. I purchased the Sig P226 Legion a few weeks after I reviewed it. Several hundred rounds later, I think this is one of the best 9mm pistols available at a reasonable price. *Review: August 3, 2017*

Kimber
Solo 9mm

The Kimber Solo is no longer in production and has been replaced by the Micro 9. The Solo was one of a few guns that I purchased without reading reviews. I liked the weight, the finish, the sights, and having a 9mm for concealed carry. The Solo is very accurate and the recoil is moderate. There are several problems with this pistol, starting with the price. If I remember correctly, I think I paid $750.00 for this four years ago. Four years ago, ammunition was expensive and, on occasion, hard to get. Kimber recommended 124 or 147-grain hollow point ammo and stated that 115-grain ammo would not recycle properly. I shoot at least two magazines a month for practice with my concealed carry pistol, and if I am not satisfied with my accuracy, I will shoot up to fifty rounds. I thought it was stupid to practice with expensive ammo because I shoot good quality 115-grain ammo. The Kimber has been in my safe for two years and I thought it was time to shoot it and review it. I decided to shoot 115-grain ammo at thirty feet with three eight round magazines and one six round magazine.

I was shooting rapid-fire minus the interruptions. On my third shot, the ejected round hit the middle of my forehead, so I stopped for a few seconds to check for blood. There were no other problems with the first magazine. The second shot of my other magazine failed to eject. In a life or death situation, say hello to Mr. Death. The third magazine had an ejection failure on the third shot, and no problem with the fourth magazine. I have read several complaints about the recycling problem with the more expensive ammo. I would never recommend anyone using the Solo as a concealed carry pistol. If it were any good, Kimber would still be manufacturing it. I will not sell or trade the Solo because I am afraid someone might use this as a concealed carry pistol. I do not recommend any videos on the Solo because they aren't worth your time to watch. *Review: June 5, 2017*

CZ
P-10 C

The CZ P-10 C is another excellent striker-fired pistol in a very crowded market. I had a two and a half month wait before I received my P-10 C because the demand usually exceeds production. I often fire one hundred rounds through any pistol before reviewing it, but I could not resist doing a quick out-of-the-box review. The initial impression is that I like the fit and finish, the sights, the great trigger, and the price. The MSRP is $500.00 and this is a great bargain. Don't expect a discount because CZ does not have a gun dealer-friendly pricing policy. The P-10 C holds 15 rounds in the magazine plus one in the chamber. I was shooting rapid fire at a target thirty feet away. My first few shots were going left, and my guess is it was me and had nothing to do with the pistol. I will review the CZ and all of my striker-fired 9mm pistols on the same day soon. I want to make notes and rank them based on my experience after firing them after one day of shooting. If you are purchasing a gun for home defense or concealed carry, shop at a gun dealer who will rent different pistols that you can shoot at their gun range before you make a choice. Several YouTube videos reviewing the P-10 C are interesting and informative. This CZ could be the best buy and the best striker-fired pistol that is available. *Review: May 25, 2017*

Bond Arms
The Texan

Fifty years ago, I traded an over and under 38 special Derringer to my dad for a 1941 German Luger that my brother, Ron, brought back from Germany at the end of World War II. I didn't like the Derringer and had no intention of ever owning another one. After fifty years, I changed my mind. I purchased a Bond Arms Texan chambered in 45 Colt or 410 shotgun shells. The quality and fun factors of this Derringer are excellent. The Texan has a six-inch barrel, and I purchased a four-and-a-half-inch barrel if I want to use it as a concealed carry. I fired two 410 00 buck with four pellets from seventeen feet and two from twenty-five feet. There is quite a change in the spread of the pellets. I fired two slugs and two 45 Colt cartridges at twenty-five feet, and I believe the 00 buck is the best for self-defense. Bond Arms engraved The Texan free as part of the promotion for the introduction of this excellent pistol. There is an excellent Hickok45 video and a Bond Arms safety video on YouTube. *Review: May 20, 2017*

Sig Sauer
1911 45ACP

The Sig 1911 is another superb handgun from Sig Sauer. There are several versions and every year the models seem to get better. My 1911 is several years old but it is still an excellent model. All of the 1911 manufacturers make a significant 45ACP. If you are buying your first 1911, I recommend trying several brands. It's like buying clothes; some brands fit each individual better than others. The pros for 1911 are that it's a historical weapon that is still great today. It's a good home defense weapon and has excellent stopping power. The ammo is inexpensive when buying 1,000 rounds as it's thirty to thirty-five cents per round. Cons: It's expensive compared to polymer pistols. The magazines hold eight to nine rounds compared to polymer 45ACPS-10 rounds. It takes a little longer to clean compared to modern polymer pistols. The 1911 was my primary weapon when I was a military policeman in the Army, and I would go to the range quite a bit because I was broke, most of the time, and ammo was free. Some like the 1911 as a concealed carry pistol, but in my opinion, there are better choices. There are YouTube videos on Sig 1911s that are informative and entertaining. *Review: May 4, 2017*

Springfield XDM 40

The XDM 40 is another excellent pistol from Springfield. The 40 caliber is a unique round that is in between the 9mm and the 45ACP. The XDMs from Springfield are available in 9mm, 40, and 45ACP calibers. I really cannot feel any difference in the recoil of the 40 and the 9. The way the XDM fits my hand is fantastic. It has several safety features, sixteen rounds in the magazine plus one in the chamber, excellent sights, minimal recoil, and is a great value. The XDM 40 is an ideal home protection pistol, and, depending on the clothes you are wearing, it could be a concealed carry. The only drawback for a 40- caliber pistol is that ammo is usually more expensive than 9mm. If you tend to shoot a lot, ammo's cost is a factor unless you reload your ammo. *Review: May 10, 2017*

Smith & Wesson
M&P 45ACP

The S&W M&P 45 is an excellent striker-fired semi-automatic pistol. It holds ten rounds plus one in the chamber, has remarkable sights, is very accurate, reliable, and is manufactured in the USA. The recoil is average and, for a full size 45, it feels good. The M&P is compared to a similar Glock model all the time. It seems like the Glock is favored over the Smith & Wesson by a good number of people comparing the pistols. I don't get it! I would take the M&P over the Glock because, in my opinion, it has a better trigger, less recoil, and feels better. I cannot tell any difference in the accuracy. Colion Noir has a funny review on YouTube on the M&P. *Review: April 19, 2017*

Stoeger
Cougar 9 MM

The Stoeger Cougar is a nice semi-auto pistol with a fifteen-round magazine. It has an excellent finish, is accurate, has mild recoil, and is priced around $375.00 to $400.00. The Stoeger Cougar is a Beretta Cougar. Benelli USA purchased Stoeger and Beretta owns Benelli. Beretta replaced the Cougar with a

PX4 Storm and sent the Cougar tooling to Turkey's Stoeger factory. The Beretta PX4 is slightly lighter than the Cougar and has a slight advantage with a better trigger. I am just as accurate with the Stoeger as I am with the PX4. Either pistol would be an excellent home protection weapon, but is kind of big for concealed carry. Usually, the PX4 is about $200.00 more than the Stoeger, but Beretta has a $75.00 rebate this month on the PX4. If you are buying a pistol just for home protection, the Stoeger Cougar would be my choice. If you are buying for home protection and range time, The Beretta is my choice. The $75.00 rebate is a game-changer. There are some excellent YouTube videos about the Cougar. *Review: April 5, 2017*

Update: I have changed my mind about either pistol being too big for concealed carry. I carry my PX4 in a Wilson Combat Hide in Plain Sight Holster.

Ruger American 9mm Pistol

I want to revisit my review of the Ruger American. This 9mm pistol is one of the great buys in today's competitive market. If you do some shopping, a reasonable purchase price is $530.00. I recently was shooting from ten yards, and after shooting two hundred rounds, I think this pistol is one of the best 9mms on the market.

Sturm, Ruger & Company is the number one manufacturer of guns in our country, and there is a good reason for them being number one. They manufacture a wide variety of reasonably priced, reliable, and quality guns that are good, very good, and excellent. In my opinion, Ruger American falls in between good and very good in an extremely competitive market. I fired three magazines (fifty-one rounds) through the American, and it is accurate, has minimum recoil, and feels good while shooting. The negatives are the trigger is okay, not great, the sights are okay, and the grips have many negative reviews about hurting the knuckle on your thumb. I did not have that problem. If I were buying one pistol in a 9mm caliber for home protection, or target shooting, it would be tenth on my list. It is strictly my opinion, and I believe this Ruger could be the number one choice for several individuals. A Hickok45 video from YouTube that is informative and entertaining and a video of the Thompson sub-machine gun history are available. If you have an interest in history, you will enjoy this video. *Review: August 17, 2019*

Springfield XDM OSP an XDM with Crimson Trace Laser

Springfield Armory is one of my favorite gun manufacturers. The company has very high-quality weapons at reasonable prices. The XDM is a very popular striker-fired semi-automatic pistol with a magazine capacity of nineteen rounds. It has moderate recoil, very accurate, and very reliable. I recently purchased an XDM with a factory-installed Vortex red dot optic. I did a comparison test with an XDM with a Crimson Trace Laser that I installed. The red dot optic has a definite advantage over the laser. The sun is not a factor for the red dot, and it is effective at a greater distance. I would rather have the laser for home protection. If a thug sees a laser on his chest, the chances are that he will run or surrender. *Review: March 13, 2017*

Sig Sauer
1911 22LR

The Sig 1911 22LR is an excellent inexpensive pistol. It is a clone for 1911 45ACP, and ammo is relatively cheap. I purchased 500 rounds from bulkammo.com for $59.00. The 1911 is not an excellent concealed carry option because of the size. The Sig could be used for home protection, but there are better options. This pistol is just fun to target shoot. It has been incredibly reliable and was a very inexpensive $450.00. I purchased the Sig four years ago, and I cannot remember having a misfire. The 1911 is an excellent introductory pistol for anyone new to shooting. There are a few short YouTube videos that are entertaining and informative.

Review: March 1, 2017

Glock
17

The Glock is an incredibly reliable pistol, and the 9mm version is enjoyable to shoot. I did a recent review on a Glock chambered in 45ACP, and that model is at the bottom of my list for 45ACP pistols. At least once a month, I practice defensive shooting. I believe in a life-threatening situation that you have time to react by pointing and shooting your pistol. If you take the time to aim, it might be a life-ending decision. This pistol is easy to disassemble and clean, decent, but not a great trigger, and not great sights. *Review: February 24, 2017*

Sig Sauer
P227 45ACP

Before I review the Sig, I want to thank my grandson Robbie's girlfriend, Monica, and the Baddish Group for sending me a bottle of Four Roses yellow-label bourbon. Monica was part of my Walther PPQ review on January 24th. I was pleasantly surprised by the gift, and I usually do not drink an 80-proof bourbon. Nice, relatively smooth whiskey. I do not drink mixed drinks, and I think this Four Roses bourbon is more at home used as a cocktail whiskey. Their single barrel and small batch are excellent whiskeys and should be enjoyed neat or on the rocks. Thanks again.

The Sig Sauer P227 is another excellent semi-automatic pistol in a very crowded market. I like the grips, the sights, and the superb build quality. It has a double-stack magazine and holds ten rounds plus one in the chamber. The Sig is one of the most enjoyable 45 ACP pistols to shoot on the range that I own. Modest recoil and is extremely accurate. There is a video on YouTube by Hickok45 that is very informative and entertaining. The only takeaway from the P227 is the price, but you have to pay for quality.

Review: January 31, 2017

Walther
P22 Pistol

The Walther P22 pistol is a great little handgun. My Walther was manufactured in Germany in the year 2013. Early models had some ejection problems because of the original magazines. The P22 is the most popular 22LR handgun in the world. The Walther is an accurate, high-quality, inexpensive pistol. The P22 can be used as a concealed carry or home protection weapon, especially for new shooters or people who just don't like the recoil of a more powerful gun. It holds ten rounds in the magazine plus one in the chamber. If you were to use this for self-defense, get defensive ammo at your local gun shop. The 22LR ammo is very inexpensive, and it is readily available. There are a few YouTube videos. One for shooting, one for disassembly, and one for recommending ammo. *Review: February 11, 2017*

Ruger
SR45

The Ruger SR45 is a striker-fired 45ACP semi-automatic pistol. The SR45 is an excellent bargain for $500.00–$550.00. Like all of Ruger's guns, the quality is superb. The SR45 is a big pistol that is very accurate, has mild recoil, and is a pleasure to shoot. Like most striker-fired pistols, the takedown for cleaning is easy. The ten-round capacity is a plus for home protection with 45ACP stopping power. I think it is too big for concealed carry. I recommend this pistol for home protection. It's also fun to shoot the gun at the range. Informative and entertaining videos about this gun are available on YouTube. *Review: January 10, 2017*

HK
P30

The HK P30 is another excellent 9mm semi-automatic pistol. The fit and finish, accuracy, reliability, and long-term value are outstanding. Heckler & Koch has a reputation for manufacturing some of the finest weapons in the world. They test new products by firing 90,000 rounds through a new gun before releasing it to the public. HK pistols are widely used in the military and police forces worldwide. Any HK is an excellent heirloom that I intend to pass on from generation to generation, and it will always be a state-of-the-art weapon. The only negative is the price. The Walther PPQ, in my opinion, does everything as well as the P30 for a few hundred dollars less. I found an excellent video on YouTube reviewing the P30 by the same person who reviewed the PPQ. I hope you enjoy the YouTube videos. *Review: January 5, 2017*

Walther PPQ

The Walther PPQ chambered in 9mm is one of my favorite pistols. I cannot find anything that I do not like about this semi-automatic, striker-fired pistol. The PPQ is very accurate, has negligible recoil, is an excellent fit and has finish. It is reasonably priced and fits your hand like a glove. One of the benefits of owning a 9mm pistol is the price of ammunition. You can purchase 1,000 rounds of PMC 115 grain on sale for $209.00. The Walther is very affordable to practice and hone your skills with any 9mm pistol, and the PPQ will not wear you out. I will review my target shooting at a later date after I install a Crimson Trace Laser. I want to compare shooting with and without the laser. There is a comprehensive review on YouTube. This pistol is worth considering if you are thinking about buying a terrific inexpensive gun. *Review: December 30, 2016*

Update: January 4, 2017. I posted a review on the Walther PPQ on December 30th and, since then, I have added a Crimson Trace Green laser to the pistol. I have posted in previous reviews about my favorable opinion of laser sights, and I thought it would be interesting to have a little experiment. Saturday, my grandson Robbie and his girlfriend Monica visited my wife and me. The purpose of the visit was to shoot as Monica is a college student in Manhattan who has never been around guns. Saturday was Robbie's third time shooting. The importance of gun safety was the first topic. Next was sighting, stance, trigger finger position, and squeezing the trigger. We started with a S&W Victory 22, and Monica did quite well. The PPQ with the laser was pretty amazing from twenty-five feet. It was a delightful afternoon and I am sure that Monica will have an interesting conversation with her parents about her range time. By the way, she also enjoyed shooting an AR-15 and was not intimidated.

Glock 41
Gen 4 45ACP

I want to start this review by telling everyone that I have no idea why I purchased this pistol. It has no practical or tactical purpose.

It was a beautiful sunny day, so I decided to shoot some handguns. I am going to give a short review of the Glock 41 Gen 4. There are several good things about this pistol. Like all Glocks, it is very reliable. I own several Glocks, and I have never had a misfire or a jammed weapon. It is not a great target gun, but you will hit your target. Now for the negative characteristics of this pistol. The recoil is more severe than any 45 that I have shot. The trigger is okay except for the pain. It tends to shoot left, and therefore I could not recommend this pistol. There are too many outstanding ones on the market. I purchased the 41 two years ago and I keep thinking that someday I will like it. Maybe when pigs fly! I recommend a YouTube video because my opinion is in the minority.

Review: October 4, 2017

Browning
Hi-Power 9mm

One of my favorite pistols is the Browning Hi-Power and, in my opinion, one of the most excellent guns that I own. The name Hi-Power is because it was the first double-stack semi-automatic with a high capacity of thirteen rounds. The fit and finish are excellent, with exceptional accuracy, and it fits a medium or small hand like it was custom made. I will write a review on the Hi-Power when my back-ordered Crimson Trace grips are released. The review will be with and without laser grips. I believe the laser grips are an excellent option for home protection and concealed carry. With or without the laser, you still have to practice for a life-threatening situation. There is an excellent Wikipedia article on Browning's involvement with the United States Marines. *Update: I fired 100 rounds through the Hi-Power, and I like the pistol, but it is antiquated compared to the modern-day 9mms. The sights and trigger are okay, but not great. I still think this is an excellent pistol with a great history. Review: December 15, 2016*

Walther
PPK/S

A Walther PPK or PPK/S is a significant historical pistol. It was designed by Carl Walther in 1929 as a PP (Police Pistol) and manufactured in 1930. Several countries used the Walther PPK for law enforcement from 1935–1992, but, like the German Luger, it was just not as good as the modern pistols. I enjoy shooting this pistol. The PPK/S fit and finish are excellent, have low recoil, and are accurate at twenty-five feet. The PPK/S is not a great concealed carry pistol. It is too big for a pistol chambered in 380 compared to the sub-compact market. Hickok45 has an excellent video on YouTube that is entertaining and informative. (This is James Bond's concealed carry for many movies.) I was fortunate to buy a limited edition model for almost the same price as the regular PPK/S. *Review: December 18, 2016*

1940 P08
German Luger

I am going to give a short review of my German Luger. This past Saturday, I fired my Luger for the first time in the last forty years. The P08 is an extremely well-made weapon with a lot of history. My brother, Ron, brought this home from World War II and I hope that this will stay in our family forever. This pistol was designed in 1898, and the reason it is named a P08 is the German Army adopted it in 1908. My only complaint about the Luger is that I am not a very good shooter with this pistol. I don't like the sights, as I am more accurate when I point and shoot instead of aiming. If I practiced, maybe I could adjust to the sights, but I doubt it. There are two excellent videos on YouTube by Hickok45 about the Luger, and the one compares with the 1911. I found both to be informative and entertaining. I posted this review in 2016, and since then, I have fired fifty rounds every year. I like the engineering of the P08, but I hate the trigger and the sights. *Review: December 9, 2016*

Sig Sauer
P238

The Sig P238 is one of the great sub-compact concealed carry pistols available at a reasonable price. The accuracy is excellent, and the recoil is very manageable. I highly recommend this with a Sig laser sight. I shot targets at thirty feet and forgot to bring an Allen wrench to make adjustments for the distance. I think I had adjusted the laser for twenty feet a couple of years ago. The small pistol has an excellent trigger pull and reset. Several very informative and entertaining videos are available on YouTube. *Review: December 6, 2016*

Smith & Wesson
M&P 40 Compact

The Smith & Wesson M&P 40 is an excellent concealed carry semi-automatic pistol. It is accurate, lightweight, and the recoil is manageable. The M&P is available in 9mm, 40, and 45ACP. The 40 stopping power is greater than the nine and less than the 45. I would not buy this or any other compact for home protection. The better choice would be a full-size pistol with less recoil and that is a lot more natural to shoot when practicing. There is a YouTube video that shows the recoil of a compact 40. *Review: November 28, 2016*

Kimber 1911
Crimson Trace Pro Carry 2

The Kimber is a great concealed carry or home defense pistol. It's lightweight, has a great fit and finish, and has a superb Crimson Trace laser. I practice rapid-fire shooting with this 1911. The laser is excellent on a cloudy day and inside a building, but it's useless in the sunlight. I practice the point-and-shoot method because you may not have time to aim in a defensive situation. There is a video demonstration of shooting this gun available on YouTube. I posted this review in 2016. The pistol is now in my single gun safe on my nightstand. *Review: November 26, 2016*

Smith & Wesson
Victory

The Victory is an excellent 22 target pistol. It has easy takedown for cleaning, the 22LR ammo is cheap, it has outstanding balance, and sights. The only drawback is 22LR ammo is dirty and you should clean all 22 pistols and rifles frequently. There is a video from YouTube by Plinkster22 comparing the Victory with the new Ruger Mark IV. Smith & Wesson, and most manufacturers have a lifetime warranty on their firearms. Last year I sent a fifty-year-old 357 Combat Magnum to S&W, and the factory repaired it at no charge, and I think they paid for shipping. I posted a review earlier in this publication with an optic. The S&W Victory is a bargain and a joy to shoot. *Review: June 9, 2019*

Kel-Tec
PMR-30

The Kel-Tec PMR-30 is a fun pistol to shoot and is also an excellent choice for home protection or concealed carry. Pro comments: it has the same velocity as a 38 special with a third of the recoil. The magazine holds thirty cartridges. Excellent sights, and weighs 13.6 ounces. The 22 Magnum ammunition is inexpensive and is very accurate. Cons: After twenty rounds, it is a pain to load the last ten rounds. I am looking at various speed loader reviews. I want to change my recommendation for home protection. Ted S. reminded me of the bright flash at night from the PMR-30 and that the thirty-shot magazine would not give you an advantage if you were temporarily blinded. I posted this review in 2016, and since then, there is an excellent speed-loader available for the PMR. *Review: November 17, 2016*

HK
VP9

The HK VP9 is another excellent 9mm striker-fired pistol. The finish, sights, trigger, grips, and reliability are exceptional. The VP9 is accurate and the price is right. The VP9 is one of my favorite pistols. HK continues to manufacture high-quality guns at reasonable prices. If I were shopping for one 9mm pistol at an affordable price, there would be three choices: the VP9, Walther PPQ, and the CZ P10 C. There is an excellent video on YouTube about this gun by Hickok45.

Review: November 10, 2016

Remington
R1 1911

Today I will review two 1911 45ACP Remington R1s. One has been customized and enhanced by Wilson Combat, and the other is stock, except it has Crimson Trace Laser grips. I tried to simulate someone who has a pistol for home protection that is not familiar with handguns or has not practiced shooting. Shooting is like any sport. If you don't practice, chances are you will not be at the top of your game. Today is the first time that I have shot a 1911 in two months. I used a cardboard target that simulates a kill zone. The first shooting was with the Wilson Combat at twenty feet. Most life-threatening situations occur from fifteen to twenty-five feet. I fired three rapid-fire shots by pointing and shooting (no target shooting techniques) and looking at the target, right shoulder, belly shot, and lower chest. Next, at fifty feet taking three-point and shoot shots and one three-second aim and shoot. Two shots missed the target, one barely nicked, and the three-second trajectory hit the lower part of the bull. Unless someone is shooting at you, never take a shot at fifty feet. The next shooting with the Crimson Trace 1911 starts with twenty feet and moves to fifty feet. Twenty feet is a good pattern for rapid-fire point and shoot. At fifty-feet, the first rapid-fire three on the target, but not close to the kill zone. The three-second aim and shoot are dead center bull. Three seconds gives you enough time to have proper finger placement on the trigger.

Finger placement on a trigger is just like swinging a golf club as a wrong placement is a hook or a slice. At fifty feet, I hooked the point and shoot shots. The reason for this comparison is that, if you are buying a pistol for home protection, an inexpensive handgun with a laser is a great option and the most sensible. R1 with laser grips approximate cost is $1,200.00- R1 enhanced and customized by Wilson Combat-$1,700.00. I would like to have some input from active or retired law enforcement. I have never been in a life-or-death situation, so this review is an educated guess. Unless someone has experienced this, who knows how each individual would respond. *Review: November 4, 2016*

Beretta
Px4 Storm

One of my favorites for a concealed carry pistol and a Wilson Combat "Hide in Plain Sight" holster is my Beretta Px4 Storm compact. The magazine holds fifteen rounds, and I take a spare in the holster. It's very accurate and has minimal recoil. Like all Beretta guns, the quality is impeccable. I have never had a misfire or any problem with this great pistol. The trigger is crisp with an excellent reset. This terrific 9mm handgun is a perfect choice. *Review: October 28, 2016*

Ruger LCP
and LCP 2

The Ruger LCP is one of the most popular concealed carry pistols in the world. There are a lot of pros and cons regarding it and I'd like to start with the pros. The LCP weighs 9.3 ounces without the loaded magazine. You can put this pistol in your pocket with an extra magazine, and you might forget that a gun is actually there. LCP is very accurate at twenty feet and reliable. I've never had a misfire or failure to eject. 380 ammo for a defensive situation is quite good and therefore I carry the LCP 80% of the time when I carry a concealed weapon. The LCP is also very inexpensive. The Cons: Most people who shoot for a living are not crazy about the 380 Cartridge for self-defense. The trigger pull is long but smooth, however the sights are not very good. The slide doesn't stay open after firing the last round.

The pros and cons of the LCP are right on the money, but if I shoot two magazines, rapid-fire per month for practice at twenty feet, and if you hit a target in the kill zone, it doesn't matter what caliber the cartridge is. My LCP has two extended magazines (seven rounds instead of six) and one in the chamber. I will not carry one in the chamber because the LCP is hammer-fired. If you drop a hammer-fired weapon without a safety, it could discharge a round. A striker-fired pistol is safe with or without a safety.

Update on Ruger's LCP 2. I purchased the LCP 2, and the improvements are: better trigger, better sights, the slide stays open after firing the last round, and the grip is much better than the LCP. *Review: May 30, 2017*

Glock
34

Glock model 34 chambered in 9mm is a good pistol, but in my opinion, not great. The trigger is good but the sights are average. The reliability is excellent but the accuracy is average. The price is on the high side in relation to the competition. I don't know why I bought several Glocks because I am not a fan.

Review: June 20, 2017

Sig Sauer
P290

The P290 is a sub-compact 9mm semi-automatic pistol that has a six-round magazine capacity. I was surprised at the low recoil of this twenty-ounce pistol. There is a lot of competition in the sub-compact field which would not be my number one choice. The gun is accurate at twenty-five feet, has excellent sights and good stopping power. The problem with this tiny gun is the disassembly. It's a pain in the ass. *Review: August 14, 2016*

Ruger
Charger 22LR

The Ruger Charger is a very unusual gun. When I saw this in a gun shop, my first reaction was, what is this and what is its purpose? Is it a rifle or a pistol? My next thoughts were: what a great gun to teach young children to shoot on a shooter's table with a bi-pod; what a great gun for someone who only has the use of one arm; what an excellent weapon for older people whose strength goes away with age. After my purchase and shooting the Charger, my impression was what a great plinker. The Ruger suggested retail is $309.00 and it comes with a bi-pod and has a Picatinny rail for mounting a red dot or a scope. I mounted the Sig Romeo red dot that was initially on one of my AR-15s. I was shooting at two targets that were thirty-five yards from my shooter's table. I first zeroed the red dot and shot with some wind: the second, no wind, and rapid-fire. I was also shooting eighteen-inch steel at 150 yards and 200 yards. Once you establish the bullet drop, it is easy at 150 yards and a lot harder at 200 yards. The Charger comes with a fifteen-round

magazine, and I purchased three twenty-five magazines through Shop Ruger. They were $33.95 each,
less the 20% off coupon that Ruger encloses in every
gun purchase. Hickok45 has an excellent video on
YouTube that is entertaining, but I wish he would have
been shooting from some type of bench because I don't
see any reason to buy the charger to shoot while you
are standing. *Review: March 31, 2017*

High-Standard
Supermatic Trophy

I purchased my High-Standard Supermatic Trophy
Pistol in 1978 or 1979. I try to shoot this excellent
target pistol two times per year. The last year that the
High-Standard was manufactured was 1984. The 22LR
firearms manufactured today have come a long way in
several areas, but the Supermatic Trophy can still com-
pete with the best. My gun features are: outstanding
balance and grip, terrific trigger, excellent sights, and

easy disassembly. I wish that I would have bought extra magazines because it's a pain shooting and reloading one magazine. *Review: October 7, 2018*

Ruger
Mark1

The Ruger Mark1 was the first gun that the Sturm-Ruger company manufactured and produced from 1949 to 1982. I purchased my Ruger in the late 1970s. The Mark1 is an excellent 22LR pistol: nice trigger, impeccable fit, finish, and adjustable rear sights. The only negative is the disassembly of this iconic gun. Compared to today's 22LR pistols, it is time-consuming. I think the popularity of this pistol started with looks and accuracy. The Mark1 kind of resembles the German Luger and the Japanese Nambu. *Review: November 4, 2018.*

III
Rifles

Ruger Precision Rifle chambered in 22LR with a Hawke 3x9x40 Vantage Scope with BDC for 22LR

I wanted to revisit this review from 2018 because this is an excellent rifle with tremendous scope, is fun to shoot, and very accurate up to 200 yards.

I recently purchased a Ruger Precision Rifle chambered in 22LR with a Hawke Vantage 3x9x40 with a BDC (bullet drop compensator) for 22LR. I have the Precision Rifle chambered in a 308Win and it is incredibly accurate. I have several 22LR rifles and pistols, but shooting beyond fifty yards is a challenge. At 200 yards, a 22LR trajectory drops over three feet, so to hit a target, you have to shoot three feet above the target. With a BDC scope, you zero at fifty yards and use the reticle scale to hit the target. I plan on teaching my grandchildren to shoot at two hundred yards with this Ruger. There is an excellent video about this gun by Plinkster22 on YouTube. *Review: May 26, 2020*

Rimfire 22LR HV 9x Reticle

Registered reticle design exclusive to Hawke. Aim points calculated for your specific caliber. Easy to zero and outstanding downrange accuracy with illuminated aim points for all lighting conditions. Distances etched into the reticle field of view, designed for use on maximum magnification.

They were designed for the .22 LR High Velocity (HV) caliber. Zero on 9x magnification at fifty yards and all aim points are pre-calculated. 1260 fps (384 m/s).

The scope can also be used for 50m zero with aim points correct in metric when the magnification is set to 7.8x.

Weatherby Vanguard Adaptive Composite 308 with a Leupold VX2 3x9x40 Scope

I posted a review on August 28th about The Weatherby VAC chambered in 223, and, after shooting the rifle, I purchased the same gun chambered in a 308. Weatherby has always produced great rifles, and, in my opinion, the VACs are incredible. I am not a hunter and I am sure this would not be a hunter's choice. The Weatherby is a great target rifle. I have made some fantastic shots at 200 yards and I am not a great shooter. Much to my chagrin, the VACs are not in the Weatherby 2018 catalog. I contacted Weatherby to ensure there was not a problem with the rifles, and the representative assured me that the gun's quality is fine. I guess the sales would not justify manufacturing the VAC for 2018. If you want a great target rifle that will not break the bank, buy one while still available. There are several YouTube videos about this rifle available. *Review: January 27, 2020*

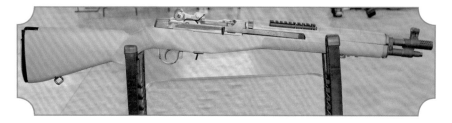

Springfield M1A
Standard and Socom

I have not fired a rifle for a couple of months due to weather, family commitments, and pistol shooting. Two weeks ago I decided to shoot my M1A standard and my M1A Socom. The M1s are terrific rifles and very reliable. They are my only rifles chambered in 308 that don't have a scope. I shoot pretty well at 150 yards, but at 200 yards, I have a problem with smaller targets. I am okay with sixteen and eight-inch steel. I hate the thought of installing a scope on an M1A, but

I think that I will buy a Scout scope for my Socom. It's not easy being an old guy. *Review: July 29, 2019*

Update: January 2, 2021, I tried a scope, but I didn't feel right shooting an M1 with a scope, so maybe I will just shoot at bigger targets.

—⦿⦿⦿—

Browning Automatic Rifle (B.A.R.)

The Browning B.A.R. has quite a history! When I was sixteen years old, I joined the National Guard. When I told the Company Commander my age, he asked the First Sergeant to take me out of the office so he could say to me my age. I came back into the office and told the Captain that I was seventeen. Enlistment accepted! I was in an Armored Recon Company, and my primary weapon was a B.A.R. Sixteen pounds of unbelievable firepower! Browning has a modern version of the B.A.R. that weighs around six or seven pounds, semi-automatic, and has a four-round magazine instead of the old military version of twenty rounds. I have read a terrific World War II novel that is the first of a Trilogy. It has some fictional characters, but the research and accuracy of the Philippines' war are outstanding. It brought back memories of carrying and firing the B.A.R. If anyone wants to read the novel *Betrayed, Deserted, and Forgotten* by Ted Snedeker, it is available on Amazon.

An excellent video of the B.A.R. by Hickok45 is available on YouTube. The genius of John Browning is unbelievable. The most famous of his firearms is the 1911. Browning designed the Winchester 1897 Pump Shotgun. Before this famous Winchester shotgun, the company was manufacturing a clumsy heavy lever-action shotgun. Excellent articles are available on the internet about John Browning. Possibly the most comprehensive report about the B.A.R. is on Wikipedia. I do not own a B.A.R., so there isn't a photo posted.

Review: January 22, 2019

Ruger Mini 14
with a Leupold 3x9x40 Scope

The Ruger Mini 14 Tactical is an excellent rifle similar to the M14 military rifle that replaced the M1 Garand. My mini is chambered in 5.56 NATO/ 223, very versatile because of the size, and weighing 6.7 pounds with an overall length of 36.75 inches. The sights are similar to the Springfield M1A, but in my opinion, not as good and a lot harder to zero. The Mini 14 has been in production since 1974, with several improvements over the years for accuracy. With the Leupold Scope, I can hit six-inch steel at 200 yards. MSRP on this Mini

14 is $1169.00, but the average purchase price is in the $1,000.00 range. I highly recommend this rifle. I posted this review on August 5, 2017. Since my August review, I have not shot the mini, and I forgot how enjoyable it was to shoot this rifle. I will be shooting the mini more frequently. The fun factor is an A+.

Review: November 25, 2018

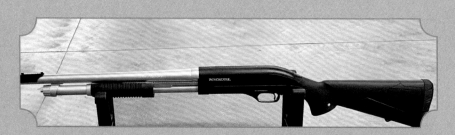

Winchester SXP 12-Gauge Pump shotgun

A few months ago, I won a Winchester SXP from a Greensburg Police raffle. What a pleasant surprise. The twelve-gauge shotgun is a great home defense or just a fun gun to shoot. I think the retail on this SXP is $400.00. I posted a previous review on a Mossberg 590A1, which is another inexpensive 12-gauge pump. In my opinion, you can flip a coin on your choice. Both are excellent affordable shotguns. There is a perfect YouTube video by Hickok45 on this rifle.

Review: June 18, 2018

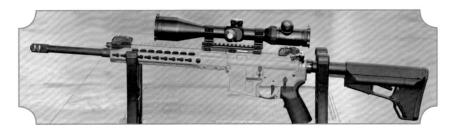

Barrett Rec7 With Hawke 4x16x50 Scope

I celebrated my seventy-eighth birthday in January by giving myself a present. I purchased a Barrett piston-operated AR-15, the Rec7 DMR (designated marksman rifle). I own three other ARS, and this will be my last AR-15 purchase. Barrett is a high-end quality rifle that is extremely accurate and reliable. I wanted to try a different scope, so I decided on the Hawke 4x16x50, and this a tremendous scope. I zeroed the scope by using a shortcut that I watched on a YouTube video. I have used the twenty-five-yard shortcut twice. Dead center at twenty-five yards, allow for a 1-1/2inch rise at 200 yards, make your adjustment at two hundred yards (one click= 1/2 inch at two-hundred yards), and it is right on the money. I save a lot of steps instead of zeroing at 100 yards. All the AR-15s are great rifles, whether they cost $600.00 or $3,000.00. There are several videos on YouTube on the Barrett. I am reposting this review because this is one of the rifles that I hope will stay in the family. The original posting was on February 7, 2017, on batesvilleshooter.com.

Update: April 14, 2018

Springfield
M1A

Hopefully, the M1A is another keeper for my children and a must for anyone who enjoys shooting rifles. Below is a past review.

The Springfield M1A is the civilian version of the military M14, which succeeded the M1 Garand. The M1 Garand was the infantry rifle during World War II, and five million rifles were manufactured during that period. The problem with the M1 was an eight-round clip and 30.06 ammunition. The M14 has a twenty-round magazine and the ammunition is 7.62x51 (the civilian equivalent is 308 Win). The 308 ammo is significantly more accurate, over two hundred yards, and the ammo is smaller and lighter than the 30.06. I purchased the Standard M1A approximately eighteen months ago, and it is a great rifle. It is incredibly reliable, has a soft recoil, and I consistently hit steel at 200 yards with factory sights. I qualified Sharpshooter with the M1 when I was in the National Guard and joined the Army. Your primary MOS (Military Operational Service) in the Army is 111 (infantry), so everyone had to qualify with the M1 during basic training. Springfield Armory has several variations of the M1A. I do not think the M1A would be the best rifle for a hunter. I think the preference would be a bolt action model with a scope. For fun and the challenge of shooting with iron sights, the M1A is my choice. There are several videos on YouTube featuring a couple of different models of the M1A.

Review: April 8, 2018

Browning X Bolt chambered in 308 with a Leupold VX2 3x9x40 Scope

The Browning X Bolt is another great rifle from Browning. I have a Browning A-Bolt chambered in 308, and the most notable difference is the trigger on the X Bolt. It's magnificent! Combined with the Leupold scope, it's very accurate at 200 yards. Every Browning that I have fired or just held, the quality is impeccable. Several videos are available on YouTube.

Review: March 19, 2018

Update: December 12, 2020. Whenever I am target shooting with my X Bolt, it makes my day. What an unbelievable inexpensive rifle!

Henry 30-30 with a Hawke 3x9x40 Scope

The Henry 30-30 is an excellent rifle in the 100 to 150-yard range. White Tail hunters like the light-weight and the stopping power of the cartridge. I am not a hunter, and most of my target shooting is 170 to 200 yards. My problem with the 30-30 cartridge is at 200 yards, the bullet drop is almost seven inches and the ammo is more expensive than a superior 308 cartridge. The Henry 30-30 with the brass receiver has an MSRP of $950.00 but the going price is $800. There are some excellent YouTube videos available about this rifle. *Review: January 14, 2018*

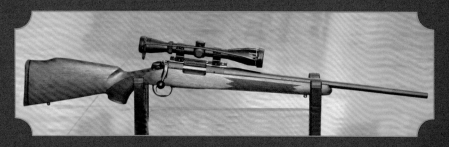

Bergara B14 Chambered in 308 with a Leupold VX2 3x9x40 Scope

The Bergara B14 is another excellent bolt action rifle in a crowded field of hunting and target rifles. Bergara is a Spanish rifle manufacturer that is known for manufacturing superior quality barrels. The B14 is a very high-quality rifle at a reasonable price. I purchased the Timber model that is about $120.00 more than the synthetic model. With Scope rings, base, and tax, my purchase price was $1,250.00. My B14 is very accurate at 200 yards and, from the reviews that I have seen and read, distances up to a mile. I have been asked by some friends and relatives to pick my favorite pistol and rifle that I own. My reply was that I could pick my top ten in each category, so when the weather gets nasty and curtails my shooting, I will pick my top ten and give my opinion on my rankings. There are several videos on YouTube that I highly recommend. I forgot to mention the trigger on the B14 is great.

Review: January 26, 2018

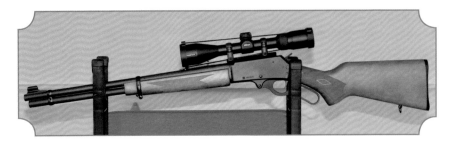

Marlin 336 chambered in 30-30Win with a Nikon 3x9x40 Scope

My last review was on the Henry 30-30, so I thought I should follow up with a Marlin review. The Marlin is a great buy. You can purchase a 336 without scope for approximately $425.00 or one with a 3x9x40 scope for under $500.00. The price is about half the price of a Henry, and it is just as accurate with an excellent trigger and smooth action. If you are looking for a nice rifle at a budget price, this Marlin is it. As I wrote in my review on the Henry, the 30-30 cartridge is for a range of 100 to 150 yards. There are excellent reviews on YouTube of this rifle. *Review: January 20, 2018*

Update: January 10, 2021. Henry purchased the rights and inventor of Marlin's gun division.

Sig Sauer 516 with Hawke 3x9x40 Scope

The Sig 516 was my second AR-15 purchase, and I think it is an excellent rifle. I have fired hundreds of rounds through it and never had a misfire. My 516 is a gas piston operating system and requires less cleaning than a direct impingement rifle. If you want accuracy, a widespread belief is not to buy a gas piston operating system AR-15. I have four AR-15s, and three are piston operating systems. My Sig is remarkably accurate at 200 yards with the Hawke scope. I do not use target grade ammo because of the price, and I am not shooting for one inch or less MOA (the measurement of a group of shots). As long as I can hit four and six-inch steel at 200 yards, I think the AR-15 is very accurate. The only problem with Piston AR-15s is that they are more expensive than the direct impingement rifles. Several YouTube videos about this gun are exciting and entertaining. *Review: January 8, 2018*

Savage Axis XP
chambered in 223

Last year I reviewed the Savage Axis XP chambered in 308. The reason that I purchased one chambered in 223 was the price, accuracy, and cost of ammo. I checked the Savage website, and with the rebate, you can buy an Axis XP for around $350.00. My last review was about the Remington 783 at a similar price point. You cannot go wrong with either of these budget rifles. I purchased the Savage chambered in 223 because it's very accurate and, since I am not a hunter, the cost of 223 ammo compared to the 308 is thirty cents per cartridge versus sixty cents. My XPs are older models and have Weaver Scopes versus the more recent models that have Bushnell scopes. I like the trigger on the Remington 783, but I prefer the scope on the Savage. I recommend both rifles for a beginner for hunting or target shooting. A hunter will opt for a 308 or similar cartridge. There are several videos on the Axis XP in 223 and 308 Caliber on YouTube. *Review: December 15, 2017*

Remington
783

The Remington 783 is an excellent rifle for the MSRP of $399.00. I purchased one three or four years ago, and I decided to shoot and review the 783 yesterday. It has been a couple of years since I spent any time shooting this rifle and I forgot how good the 783 is. There are a couple of negatives. The scope that is part of the 783 packages is not very good. It's accurate at 200 yards, but not precise. The bolt is a little stiff. The positives are, great trigger! Great accuracy. My 783 is chambered in 308, and Remington has a $40.00 rebate on the 783s. If you want an inexpensive rifle, you can purchase one for about $350.00. If someone is purchasing a 783 to be their hunting rifle, I would probably get rid of the 3x9x40 scope that is part of the purchase price and buy a Hawke or similar scope for $100.00 to $125.00. There are some excellent videos on YouTube about this gun. *Review: December 9, 2017*

Henry Big Boy
357 Magnum

I have reviewed the Henry Long Ranger chambered in 308 and the Henry Big Boy chambered in 44 Magnums. The Henry 357 is very similar to the 44 Magnum and like the 44, it has a very low recoil, it's a great shooter at fifty to one hundred yards, there's an excellent finish, and is made in America. The real advantage of the 357 over the 44 Magnum is the cost of ammo. You can purchase 1,000 rounds of 357 Magnum for around thirty cents per round, while the 44 Magnum ammo is around sixty cents per round. If you are buying a hunting rifle, my preference would be a bolt action rifle with a scope chambered in 308. There are several videos on YouTube about all the Henry rifles and the company. *Review: December 21, 2017*

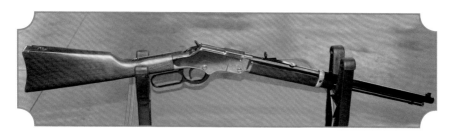

Henry Golden Boy
22LR/ S

Like all Henry lever-action rifles, the Golden Boy chambered in 22LR or 22- short is a high-quality rifle. It is at the high end for the price of a 22 rifle. The MSRP is $550.00, but the going price is $400.00–$450.00. The lever action is smooth and the sights are good. I fired a couple of rounds from twenty yards, and they were in the bullseye. At thirty-five yards, I was not hitting the bullseyes consistently because of the sun, old eyes, and the wind. At fifty yards, I hit six-inch steel with every round, which was around fifty. I did not attempt to lob any rounds at 200 yards because of the wind. There are excellent videos from YouTube on this rifle. All Henry rifles are made in America and are usually kept in the family forever. *Review: November 28, 2017*

Weatherby Vanguard Adaptive Composite Rifle with a Leupold VX2 4x12x40 Scope

The Weatherby Vanguard Adaptive Composite rifle is another great Weatherby product. I like my Weatherby that is chambered in 223 so much that I am buying another one chambered in 308. The VAC is a long-range rifle design, but, with my limited range, I can only say for me, it is incredibly accurate and fun to shoot at two hundred yards. The rifle's grip and feel are terrific, and it has an adjustable stock and cheek rest. The VAC would not be my choice for a hunting rifle because of the weight. *Review: August 28, 2017*

Ruger Precision Rifle with a Hawke 4x12x50 Scope

My Ruger Precision Rifle is a great rifle that is very inexpensive compared to most precision rifles from various manufacturers. Mine is chambered in 308 because it is a great round and affordable compared to the 6.5 Creedmoor and other powerful rounds as I have said in previous reviews. The RPR is an ideal bench rifle, not a hunting rifle, because of the weight. The trigger is superb, and the accuracy at 200 yards is excellent. I use PMC Bronze that sells for about sixty cents per round when you purchase 500 rounds. There are excellent videos on YouTube that are entertaining and informative. I like this rifle more than the LWRC Sniper rifle that sells for about three times the Ruger's price. *Review: September 9, 2017*

Ruger SR-762 with a Leupold VX2 4x12x40 Scope

After extensive research over the past few years on AR-10s, chambered in 308, which is the big brother of an AR-15, I finally purchased one. The Ruger SR-762, in my opinion, has the quality and price that is as good as it gets. I do not have the range to test it beyond two hundred yards, so it is perfect for my needs. The Leupold VX2 scope is a terrific scope at a reasonable price. There are excellent videos about this rifle on YouTube. The AR15s and the AR-10s are both great rifles. The significant differences are the price, ammunition cost (1,000 rounds of 223 are about thirty cents per round, and the 308 is about sixty cents per round), and the AR-15 magazine holds thirty rounds. The AR-10 magazine has twenty rounds, and the 308 cartridge is a more powerful round, and the recoil is almost non-existent on an AR-15. *Review: August 10, 2017*

LWRC Rapid Engagement Précision Rifle

The LWRC REPR is a sniper rifle. It is chambered in 308 and is extremely accurate. I want to thank Mike at Guns and Tackle in Greensburg, Indiana, for allowing me to shoot and review this rifle. I was shooting six-inch steel at 200 yards with ease, equipped with a Hawke 4x12x50 scope. The REPR is a rifle that the pros shoot at a thousand yards. I don't have the facility or the ability to shoot at 1,000 yards unless someone zeroed the scope for me, and I had a terrific spotter. There are excellent videos on YouTube about this high-quality sniper rifle. *Review: August 2, 2017*

Mossberg 590 Shockwave

I am posting a review on the Mossberg 590 Shockwave, and, in my opinion, this is not a gun for everyone. It is a kind of foolish purchase but it is fun to shoot. If you have an extra $450.00 and you do not mind waiting a couple of months, this Mossberg is a conversation piece and has devastating results at close range. I shot four rounds of 00 Buck with nine pellets at fifteen feet and at that distance, it leaves a hole a little bigger than a half-dollar. There is an excellent Hickok45 video of the Shockwave available on YouTube. *Review: July 10, 2017 Update: November 8, 2020. I changed my opinion on the Shockwave. This small 12- gauge pump shotgun using Double 00 Buck or slugs will make an excellent home defense gun.*

CZ 12 Gauge Coach Gun

The CZ Coach Gun is a blast from the past. The shotgun rider on stagecoaches had a double barrel 12- gauge sawed-off shotgun known as a coach gun. My CZ is not a very practical shotgun, but it is enjoyable to shoot. In the future, I will probably shoot in cold weather only. The CZ has a steel butt plate and, it kicks like a mule when shooting slugs or 00 Buck. It is more fun to shoot while wearing a puffy winter jacket than wearing a T-shirt. I posted some photos on my website. There are also videos on YouTube on the Coach Gun. The

quality of this Coach Gun is excellent. *Review: June 15, 2017.*
Update: December 10, 2020. When I purchased this shotgun, Mike at Guns and Tackle asked me if I wanted to buy a pad because of the recoil. I told him that I never fired a rifle or shotgun that I was bothered by the recoil. I shot six rounds of 00 Buck and four rounds of slugs, and the next day I had this nice-looking purple shoulder. I bought a pad!

Ruger
10-22 Rifle

I usually will not buy any limited edition of any product, but I made an exception and purchased a limited-edition Ruger 10-22 Trump Edition. The production is forty-five per state, and Guns and Tackle in Greensburg, Indiana, reserved number forty-five. It should be a wonderful heirloom for the family. The Ruger 10-22 has been around for a long time with the sale of five million-plus. I fired fifty rounds of CC standard ammo on a damp, windy day, and I will install a red dot or an inexpensive scope on this rifle. It is probably me, but I did not do well with the factory sights at fifty yards. I fired five rounds with the 10-22 rifle at two hundred yards and hit nothing. I fired two shots with my Charger and hit twelve-inch steel twice. I allowed for a forty-one-inch drop on each Ruger that I shot. The Ruger 10-22 is an excellent, inexpensive rifle that sells for about $220.00. The Trump Limited Edition was around $600.00. There are excellent YouTube videos on the 10-22. *Review: April 30, 2017. Update: June 10, 2017. I purchased a Hawke 3x7x32 Scope, and the Ruger is now super accurate.*

Henry Big Boy
Carbine 44 Magnum

The Henry 44 Magnum is an excellent lever action carbine. The finish is beautiful with a walnut stock and is very accurate at 100 yards. The sights are okay and, in my opinion, are better than the Winchester carbine sights. The lever action is very smooth, and the recoil is more than acceptable. I own several Henrys, and I like all of them, but my favorite is the Henry Long Ranger chambered in 308. I am not a hunter, but I think the 44 Magnum would be excellent at fifty to 100-yard shots. If you are buying a rifle to shoot at a range and do not reload your ammo, there are better choices because the 44 Magnum ammo is expensive. I have been shooting 240 grain Magic Tech and American Eagle, and the cost is around one dollar per round. PMC 180 grain cost $340.00 for 500 rounds (.68 per round). When shooting 240-grain ammo, there is a 2.2-inch rise at 100 yards and a fourteen-inch drop at 200 yards, and my guess is the 180 grain would be about a twenty-inch drop at 200 yards. The cost of 500 rounds of 308 PMC $319.00(.64 per round) and the trajectory has a 2.7-inch rise at 100 yards and 1.7 rises at 200 yards. Another excellent choice is an AR15 or a Ruger Mini 14 in a 223-or 556 Cartridge. PMC 223 cost $299.00 per 1,000 rounds. Very accurate at 100, 200 yards, and beyond. My advice to anyone buying one rifle is to talk to your local gun dealer, go to a range, and try out anything you are interested in buying. If that isn't possible, read reviews posted by people who own guns that you are interested in buying. There are excellent videos on YouTube shooting the Henry Big Boy Carbine 44 Magnum. *Review: April 24, 2017*

Winchester 94AE Short Barrel 30-30 with Loop Lever

The Winchester Model 94 has been manufactured since 1894 and is truly a part of American history. I have owned the 94AE for several years, and there are some real pros and cons. The pros: Part of the old West. Smooth lever action! The short barrel is lighter and easier to carry for hunters and ranchers. Loop is excellent if you are wearing gloves, and it is faster-ejecting rounds. The Cons: Expensive. The 30-30 cartridge, in my opinion, is dead. 30-30 ammo is costly. I was shooting Federal 170 grain ammo yesterday, and twenty rounds cost $25.00. PMC 308 costs $13.00 for twenty rounds and, in my opinion, is a better cartridge. The 30-30 is pretty flat for 100 to 150 yards, and it has a considerable drop beyond 150. The sights are awful. Winchester, Henry, Marlin, and some other manufacturers have great lever-action rifles chambered in various calibers. Unless you want to own a gun chambered in a historical cartridge, there are better choices. I forgot one pro. The 94AE is fun to shoot. It is loud, has a strong recoil, and you have to compensate for crappy sights. There are some videos on the Winchester 94 that are informative and entertaining on YouTube. Check out the video about the Dalton

Gang's last bank robbery that took place two years before the 1894 Winchester was manufactured. They were dumb ass criminals. *Review: April 14, 2017*

Savage10 FCP-SR 308 with a Leupold VX2 3x9x40 Scope

The Savage 10 FCP-SR is an excellent rifle. The suggested retail is $785.00, and the average selling price is $650.00 to $700.00. With a decent scope, one thousand dollars will buy a terrific rifle. The Savage is exceptionally accurate, and it has an Accu-Trigger and Accu-Stock. I think the trigger has a two-pound pull. The SR stands for suppressor ready. I have not shot anything with a suppressor and I probably won't until the government changes their stupid policy of waiting five days and paying a two-hundred-dollar fee to be able to purchase one. Earplugs are great! Sunday was a great day to shoot. It was warm and a bit windy off and on. I was shooting the Savage and a couple of AR-15s, and if I didn't have to police two hundred rounds of brass and paint the steel targets, it would have been very relaxing. If anyone is in the market for a 308, this is definitely worth your consideration. Several YouTube videos are entertaining and informative.

Review: April 10, 2017

Henry Long Ranger 308 with a Leupold 3x9x40 Scope

I am a fan of Henry rifles and the 308 cartridges. Henry is a great company that builds quality rifles and every component is made in America. I own five different Henry rifles and enjoy shooting every one of them. The Long Ranger is very accurate, fit, and the finish is excellent. The Leupold VX2 is perfect for me. If you have read some of my previous reviews, you know that I am not a hunter and my rifle range is only two hundred yards. I shoot all my rifles on a Caldwell shooters table because I am too old to shoot from a prone position and not a good enough marksman to shoot from a standing position. Henry rifles are like owning a piece of the old West and hopefully will stay in families as heirlooms. I recommend a Henry Company video that is interesting and entertaining and also a Hickok45 video from YouTube. *Review: March 18, 2017*

HK
416

The HK 416 is a 22LR AR-15 clone and is a very high-quality rifle manufactured by HK. I purchased this rifle three or four years ago, and a friend of mine had one and told me that he fired four thousand rounds through his HK before cleaning it without any misfires. I listened, but I thought you could not fire a thousand rounds of 22 without misfires. 22LR is dirty ammunition. I was wrong! I went through about three thousand rounds without a misfire before I cleaned it. My HK is a great rifle to train young people to shoot an AR-15 without recoil and an inexpensive ammo cost. I started with a very affordable red dot Sig and changed to an illuminated red and green reasonable Sig scope. YouTube has informative and entertaining videos. *Review: January 13, 2017*

Sig Sauer 716 with a Nikon 4x12x40 Scope

A few months ago, I zeroed a friend's Sig 716 with a Nikon 4x12x40 scope. The 716 is an AR-10 that is precisely like an AR15, except chambered in 308. The 716 is a gas piston-operated rifle and is very easy to clean. It is very accurate at 200 yards, and the scope is a $200–$250 bargain and performs quite well. The only negative for me is the trigger and it is not that bad. I prefer bolt action models in the 308 cartridges. I have a Sig AR-15 and will review it in the future. Several videos are available on YouTube about the 716. *Review: January 2, 2017*

Winchester XPR 308 with Hawke 4x12x40 Scope

The Winchester XPR is another fine bolt action rifle that will not break the bank. I am addicted to 308 bolt action rifles, and I have several different brands and like all of them. The XPR is very accurate, great fit and finish, and manageable recoil. The Hawke 4x12x40 scope has a blue and red illuminated reticle and is a great buy. There is a Winchester Company video celebrating its 150th anniversary on YouTube. I found it quite interesting as the video takes us through time. They are advertising the company. Winchester survived two of the biggest blunders that any other manufacturer would have probably gone out of business. The first mistake was not to compensate Benjamin Henry, who developed the company's repeating rifle, so he quit and started his own company. The second mistake was breaking ties with John Browning, responsible for designing some of the greatest weapons in history that we are still using today. *Review: December 13, 2016*

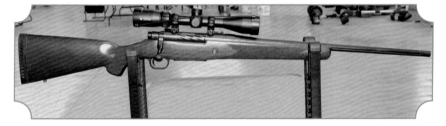

Mossberg Patriot with Vortex Scope

Mossberg is an American manufacturer who makes excellent guns at a very reasonable price. The Patriot chambered in 308 is a fine bolt action rifle. The combo with the Vortex 3x9 scope is available for around $500.00. I like this rifle's quality, but I prefer the Ruger American and the Savage Axis XP. If you will buy one rifle for hunting or shooting for sport, I recommend talking to your local gun shop about the different rifles' pros and cons and watching some video reviews on YouTube. I published this review on December 4, 2016. I recently checked my scope for zero and shot forty rounds at 200 yards. It has been over a year since I had the rifle out of my safe and forgot how good this rifle is. I can't believe the quality of this rifle for the money. This Vortex scope is not the best, but for the money, it's hard to beat. I didn't miss anything at 200 yards shooting forty rounds. *Review: November 16, 2018*

Christensen Arms
CA15 Recon

The CA15 Recon is a custom-built AR-style rifle. The piston gas system keeps the bolt running clean and cool while the carbon fiber barrel and handguard reduce weight and increase accuracy. The Recon is one of my favorite rifles. Its quality is incredible, but it is expensive. With an inexpensive AR-15 and scope, you will hit at 200 yards, just about as good as the CA15. *Review: November 14, 2016*

Browning A-Bolt3
with Redfield 3x9 Scope

Browning A-Bolt 3 with a Redfield 3×9 scope is another quality product from an excellent company. I zeroed the A-Bolt at 100 yards after seven shots. It has an excellent trigger, quality scope, and very accurate. Hard to miss at 200 yards. It's an inexpensive quality rifle! *Update: Leupold purchased Redfield, and I think Redfield manufactures scopes with Leupold glass. The scope on my A-Bolt is excellent. Review: October 28, 2016*

Mossberg 590A1
12 Gauge Shotgun

I hit an eighteen-inch steel target at two hundred yards with a slug—one out of five shots, not too shabby! I still can't believe it. I quit while I was ahead. The 590A1 is the choice of many law enforcement agencies, and it is also a terrific home protection firearm. The Mossberg is a great inexpensive shotgun that feels good, has decent sights, and manageable recoil. *Review: October 28, 2016*

Savage Axis 308 with Weaver 3x9x40 Scope

One of my great bargains rifles is the Savage Axis. The photo is a Savage Axis XP equipped with a Weaver 3x9x40 scope and sells for about $420.00. It is chambered in 308 and is very accurate at 200 yards. If I were buying a rifle for hunting, I would buy the Savage instead of a $1,000.00–$2,000.00 rifle. There is a YouTube video by mrgunsngear that is very informative. I have fired this rifle quite a bit and I consistently hit four-inch steel at 200 yards and have never lost zero on this scope. *Review: October 28, 2016*

Smith & Wesson M&P 15-22 with Sig Sauer Scope

The Smith & Wesson 15-22 is another excellent AR15 clone chambered in 22LR. The M&P is a very light, accurate rifle at fifty yards. It's okay at 100 yards on a calm day. I have a Sig inexpensive red/ green dot scope installed on the rifle that makes it a pleasure to shoot. My previous review on the HK chambered in 22LR manufactured by Walther is still my favorite of the two. The S&W is lighter, less expensive, and also very reliable. It is a fun day when you can go through 500 rounds of 22LR for under fifty dollars. I have posted YouTube videos of me shooting this rifle that are very entertaining. *Review: February 8, 2018*

Weatherby Vanguard 308 with a Leupold VX2 3x9x40 Scope

The Weatherby Vanguard 308 is one of my favorite rifles. It has minimal recoil for a 308 and has an accurate outstanding trigger. It's a high-quality rifle that is inexpensive. The Leupold VX2 scope is excellent! Leupold manufactures their scopes in America, the glass is superb and is easy to zero. I zeroed this scope with a tip from a YouTube video and am usually not impressed by shortcuts, but this one worked. You start by getting dead center at twenty-five yards. A 5.56 or 308 will rise an inch and a quarter to inch and a half at 100 yards, so one-click equals a quarter of an inch at 100 yards, and four clicks at twenty-five yards will equal the quarter-inch at 100. After I zeroed at twenty-five yards, I went twenty-four clicks down and my first shot hit four-inch steel at 200 yards. The 308 from 100 to 200 yards is pretty flat. I continued the rest of my session hitting steel at 100, 150, and 200 yards. I was impressed with the shortcut. I will use this on my next rifle to see if I was lucky or if this method is so simple that I will never go back to my old, slow ways to zero. A video is available from Weatherby for hunters, and I enjoyed the scenery and the hunt. I never had the opportunity to hunt when I was young as I grew up in the city as part of a lower-middle class family and feel I am too old to start now. I turned seventy-eight yesterday. I hope you hunters will post a review on the site of one of your favorite hunts and one of your favorite rifles.

Review: January 21, 2017

Wilson Combat AR-15 Recon Tactical with a Primary Arms 1x6x24 Raptor Scope

Wilson Combat manufactures excellent high-end weapons, and the Recon Tactical is a superb AR-15 for military and law enforcement. My Wilson has an EOTECH holographic sight, which is perfect for quick acquisition and ideal for law enforcement and the military. The Recon is very reliable, accurate, expensive, and a dumb purchase. I am seventy-eight years old, and I shoot from a shooter's bench so I don't need the tactical rifle and non-magnified sight. My Sig AR-15 is a piston-operated AR-15 with a Nikon 4x12 scope with great accuracy and less maintenance than the Wilson. The piston-operated AR-15s require minimal cleaning compared to the direct impingement AR-15s. I purchased this Wilson four or five years ago and, for less money, I could have bought a Ruger 308 with a piston AR platform and an excellent scope for less than I paid for the Wilson EOTECH combo. Live and learn. There is a Wilson AR-15 video and two EOTECH videos available on YouTube. *Review: June 10, 2017*

Update: November 20, 2020, I installed a Primary Arms 1x6x24 Raptor on my Wilson Combat. The Raptor is a magnificent scope, and I installed my EOTECH on my CZ Scorpion. An unbelievable improvement for both guns.

IV

Accessories,
Shooting Aids,
and Advice

I want to start this section by explaining why I refer to YouTube in so many of my reviews. If a person is new to firearms, the YouTube channel has a lot of information and opinions on guns by people who, in my opinion, are experts. They make their living on that channel. For instance, if you purchased a new firearm and want to learn how to clean the gun, you type the word "cleaning" in the search box. Below I am listing some of my favorite channels on YouTube and also on Full30.

Hickok45 has 5,035,000 subscribers on YouTube and 43,651 on Full30. The reason for his unbelievable popularity is his stellar ability to review guns for the novice and also the expert. He is very knowledgeable about all manner of firearms. His videos are also entertaining; in several he demonstrates the various ways to obliterate a variety of fruits and vegetables using different firearms.

Jerry Miculek has 1,034,000 YouTube subscribers. Jerry has a great personality and is one of the all-time greatest shooters. His speed and accuracy shooting revolvers, pistols, and rifles is uncanny. He has eleven world records and over 100 national and world titles. His videos are also a lot of fun to watch.

Plinkster22 has 653,000 YouTube subscribers and 16,099 Full30 subscribers. He has a great personality, does incredible trick shots, and is very informative. One of his more entertaining videos demonstrates how many Little Debbie snack cakes will a 22LR go through. Watch the video to find out!

Iraqveteran8888 has 2,042,000 YouTube sub-scribers and 30,104 Full30 subscribers. Both of his channels are incredibly informative, very entertaining, and factual. He also reviews body armor by way of firearm tests.

Mrgunsngear has 485,000 YouTube subscribers and 22,659 Full30 subscribers. His channel is informative, entertaining, and technical.

Sootch00 has 1,003,000 YouTube subscribers and 26,515 Full30 subscribers. Sootch00 channels are informative, entertaining, and technical.

Military Arms has 1,009,000 YouTube subscribers and 34,829 Full30 subscribers. The Military Arms Channel has 1,022 videos with an incredible number of different firearms.

Anyone who has an interest in guns should enjoy the videos that are available on YouTube and Full30. It's hard to watch the crap on television and the movies that are available to the public.

∽∽∽

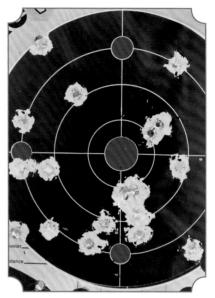

Practice,
Practice, Practice!

Today was a beautiful day to shoot. I have not shot a handgun since December because I finally published my book, *My Quest for Life, Liberty, and the Pursuit of Happiness; 1939–2019*. January and February, and March, I have been busy selling the book. Today's range time was shooting 1911s, and it's been over seven months since I fired a 1911. A Wilson Combat, a Sig Sauer, and my Colt Gold Cup Match, which I purchased in the 1980s, were my weapons of choice. I posted some targets to emphasize the need to practice setting the targets at twenty-four feet. The average distance in a defensive situation is seventeen to twenty-one feet and I practice by shooting at one to two second intervals. The first target was shooting my Wilson Combat. The Wilson is an expensive 1911 that is a very accurate

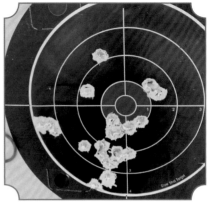

pistol, and therefore I started off shooting left. The next target was shooting the Sig, the third target was shooting the Colt, and the last was the Wilson Combat. Notice the difference in the first and final target. Practicing could save your life. *Review: March 31, 2020*

Home
Security

We live in a crazy world today, and the number of home invasions is increasing dramatically! Nationally an

alarming number of home invasions are directed at the elderly population. Through research and sound advice over the years, I have some tips that might be useful: have an alarm system with signs strategically placed in your yard. If you are home during the day, set the alarm. Remember that the thug breaking into your home will not knock on the door. My next tip is lighting is a burglar's worst enemy at night. Also, never leave things outside that could be used by the criminal, such as a ladder, hammer, etc. Close the blinds, shades, or curtains at night. I know this doesn't appeal to everyone, but get training on firearms and have home protection. There is an appropriate joke that pertains to this. A lady called 911 and said someone was breaking into her home. The 911 operator asked her if she had a gun in the house. The lady said, "No, I don't believe in guns." The 911 operator responds, "I hope you believe in God because the police are ten minutes away." I posted a few photos of my security system at home. If anyone is interested in gun safety and training, I try to give a couple of classes a year. So contact me on Facebook messenger if you'd like to take a class. *Review: April 8, 2019*

My New Concealed Carry Pistols

I've changed my primary concealed carry pistols. I purchased two DeSantis leather holsters on Cyber Monday and saved 30%. I usually drop a Ruger LCP (380) in my pocket for convenience. It holds six rounds, but beyond twenty feet it's not very accurate. Two of my favorite handguns are the Sig Sauer P226 Legion and Beretta 92FS, customized by Wilson Combat. The accuracy magazine capacity for these 9mm guns are excellent. The Legion holds 15+1 and the Beretta 17+1. They are incredibly accurate at thirty feet, and I am very comfortable shooting at thirty yards. *Review: December 15, 2018*

Range Work
with Steel Targets

I have a 200 yard rifle range and I try to maintain it every three weeks if I shoot once a week on the rifle range. I have some targets at 150 yards and 175 yards. I use AR500 steel that will handle cartridges up to and including 308Win. The steel will last forever but painting is a necessity so the steel will not rust. If you have enough property to have a safe shooting range, I highly recommend steel over paper and cardboard targets. If you need any suggestions to set up an outdoor range, I would be glad to share my experience. You can leave a comment on my website larryreidy.net.

Review: December 5, 2018

Choosing One Gun for Home Defense and Concealed Carry

Choosing one pistol or revolver for home protection and concealed carry is a tough decision. One of my daughters, Laura, wants a one do-it-all type gun. Laura, my grandson, Robbie, and his girlfriend, Monica, spent a few hours yesterday at my shooting range. Laura has shooting experience and she does quite well with 9mms. I let her shoot several of my 9mms that I consider the right mix to help her decide on a firearm soon. The pistols that she shot were a CZ75 compact, a CZ P10C, a Ruger American, a Walther PPQ, an HK VP9, a Sig Legion, a Wilson-Beretta Brigadier, and a Springfield XD. Two of her favorites, the Legion and Brigadier, were eliminated due to the price. I think she will choose either the CZ P10C or the Ruger American. Both are excellent quality for about $500.00. My grandson Robbie's concealed carry is a Smith & Wesson 9mm. We shot about 400 rounds, and it's always an enjoyable day practicing shooting with family. *Review: November 5, 2018*

Home
Defense Options

Home defense options are whatever you are comfortable with and if children still live at home or visit. I know people who have AR-15s, 12-gauge shotguns, and various handguns. I have a nightstand with a safe, and until yesterday, my home defense pistol was a Glock 26. The 26 is a tiny 9mm with a fifteen round magazine and a ten-round magazine. My Glock was ready to shoot with the fifteen-round magazine and one in the chamber and the spare ten-round magazine in the safe. I felt very comfortable with twenty-six rounds available, and until yesterday I did not consider any change. Yesterday was a great day to shoot—the temperature was in the fifties and there was little wind. I have six 1911s and decided to target shoot all of them. My new home defense pistol is my Kimber 1911 Crimson Trace Pro Carry 2. The reason for the change is accuracy at thirty feet. It was a sunny day yesterday, but the green laser was unbelievable. I used two hands, one hand, and shooting from the hip, and destroyed the bullseye. In a defensive situation, I believe that if a thug sees a laser on his chest, he will have a change of heart and surrender instead of leaving my home in a body bag. *Review: October 22, 2018*

Choosing
the Right Scope

I own several rifles with scopes that are more than adequate for me! I am not an expert marksman, but I can hit various steel sizes at my 200-yard range with the proper scope. There are so many excellent scopes on the market; it is challenging to choose the right one. If I were a hunter, a 1x6x24 Primary Arms or a 3x9x40 Hawke would do an excellent job up to 300-yards, and you are in the $150.00 to $300.00 price range. Target shooting for me at 200 hundred yards makes it easy to choose for quality and affordability. Most of my scopes are Leupold VX2s! It has excellent optics, is made in America and, depending on the power, is $250.00–$350.00 (3x9x40 or 4x12x40). I also have some Hawke scopes, not the same quality as Leupold, but priced at about $125.00 less. For the long-range shooters, 600 to 1,000 yards, go to YouTube and watch some video reviews. Some shooters will pay $2,500.00 to $3,000.00 for a scope if they are really into long-range shooting. If you are buying your first scope, check out your local gun shop. Your average gun shop will stock a few different scopes and will help you make an excellent choice. YouTube videos are very informative. *Review: August 4, 2018*

Caldwell
Stable Table

The Caldwell Stable Table is a great shooting accessory, especially for older people. There are three basic shooting positions for target shooting with a rifle. (1) The prone position. I am too old for that and have no desire to get in shape to lie on the ground. (2) The standing position. After a few shots standing, I am not steady enough to hit targets consistently. (3) The sitting position. I am in Heaven here. I have two Caldwell Stable Tables. One stays on my shooter's deck year-round and after three years is still in excellent condition—the other one for shooting at one hundred yards and cleaning rifles is in my Morton Building. I installed locking casters on both to wheel the one out of the building and kept the other locked down on the shooting deck. I have the Caldwell seat adjusted for me and when I have guests, they can use one, two, or three-inch wooden blocks to change the rifle rest. Several excellent shooter tables are available but I chose the Caldwell for the price, quality, and quick assembly and disassembly. *Review: February 27, 2018*

Bighorn Ultimate Access Gun Safe

In case anyone is considering buying a first or an additional safe, I thought I should share my thoughts and my latest safe purchase. There are excellent gun safes available from

inexpensive to really expensive prices. My first purchase was a Liberty Fat Boy, which is a superb safe manufactured in America. The Fat Boy is a large safe that I set up for a handgun safe. The next safe was a Sports Afield purchased from Costco. I think the price was around $600.00 with free delivery. I bought this safe to provide secure rifle storage, but it was too small for

a growing collection. Next was another Liberty intermediate size safe. My final safe purchase was Bighorn. It's my last safe or my wife will have me committed. The Bighorn is one giant safe with unbelievable storage. The dimensions are 71"H x 44" W x 26" D and weighs one thousand pounds. I purchased this from Costco for $1,995.00 delivered. If you are buying a first safe and have no intention of having a gun collection, buy a small, inexpensive safe. If you have the room and you are going to add to your gun collection over some time, I think the Bighorn from Costco is the best buy for a large safe. I am posting photos of my safes and I hope this will give anyone interested in buying a safe an idea on the availability of excellent gun safes.

Review: January 2, 2018

Honor
Flight

This post has nothing to do with guns, but I would like to share an experience with you. Yesterday, I had one of the most satisfying experiences of my life, joining sixty-nine other veterans on an Honor Flight. The average age was eighty-four, and the oldest vet was ninety-seven. We visited all the memorials and watched the changing of the guard at the Tomb of the Unknown Soldier. I will never forget the experience as well as being in the company of amazing people, including the guardians. Every veteran had a guardian, and my daughter Julie was my guardian. We had nine

World War II Veterans on our flight, and I have to say something about our Greatest Generation. I have always thought that if it weren't for George Washington and his citizens who became his Army, we would be having tea and crumpets instead of a beer at Happy Hour. They saved our country! The Greatest Generation consisted of the men and women who served in the Armed Forces and stayed at home keeping the factories running during World War II. THEY SAVED THE WORLD! I hope some young people read this and think about the sacrifices made by other generations so they could have a great life. Maybe they will understand why people like me will never understand or do anything to support anyone who disrespects our country. *Review: September 27, 2017*

Ladies Day
at the Shooting Range

I want to share an event that I had Saturday at my shooting range. My daughter Laura and three of her friends came to learn and shoot. Laura is the only one that has experience with shooting firearms. We started the session by reading a gun safety pamphlet and followed up with a short discussion of proper gun handling. The next step was range time. We started with a Smith & Wesson Victory 22 shooting at a paper target. Each lady fired ten rounds, and they did quite well, shooting targets from twenty-four feet. The next step was firing a Springfield XDM 9mm. They each fired two magazines (thirty-eight rounds) at a silhouette target and did very well. Their confidence grew with each shot. I demonstrated shooting a Smith & Wesson Governor with 410 Shotgun 00 buck with four pellets. They each fired one shot and I was pleasantly surprised that they were not intimidated. I asked if anyone would like to shoot an AR-15. They reacted as if someone asked them to go to their first prom. They did exceptionally well, firing my Barrett AR-15 at targets 200 yards away.

Every household should have a gun for home protection. Periodically, I will have a class for women. I posted some photos from that class. On the previous page photographed from left to right are Laura, Michelle, Susan, and Ellen.

On this page in the first photo, top left, Michelle is firing the XDM. In the second photo, top right, Ellen is firing the Governor. The third photo, bottom left, Susan is firing the AR-15. In the last photo, bottom right, Laura is firing the AR-15.

Review: May 15, 2017

Bullseye
Camera System

The Bullseye Camera System is an excellent tool for zeroing a scope. I purchased the 300-yard system a few months ago, and it saves a lot of walking. A short video is available from the company, and it is an easy setup. *Review: November 23, 2016*

Update: January 15, 2021. I used the Bullseye Camera System three times and put it on a shelf where it has stayed for the past four years. It was fun to watch on my iPad in real time the exact location of my shots at 200 yards until a bullet ricocheted off a steel target and put a hole in my battery. My next optic spotter was the Celestron Ultima 80. This spotter scope has decent glass, but it is challenging to maintain the position on the target at full power. I finally decided on Leupold 10x50 binoculars. Quick target acquisition, excellent glass, and more than adequate power for 200 yards.

Four Tips
for Better Accuracy

Consistency is a significant factor when shooting with tight groups at the rifle range: weather conditions, familiarity with your firearm, total concentration, and a steady position.

When I am shooting from the bench, I steady my rifle with either a tripod or sandbags. I always shoot a couple of rounds away from the target before I go for target acquisition. *Review: October 28, 2016*

Zeroing
a Scope

I have a tip for anyone buying a rifle with a scope for the first time. I tried different shortcuts to zero in a scope in the past, and some do not work. The proper method is zero at twenty-five yards, fifty yards, and 100 yards. Several scopes have a scale or BDC (bullet drop compensator) for longer distance shots. I usually take a shortcut. When I zero a scope at twenty-five yards, four clicks equals 1/4 inch. I shoot at sixteen inch steel at 200 yards and adjust the scope. At 200 yards, one-click equals a ½ inch. Another easy method involves a purchase of a bore-sighter. I advise you to watch a YouTube video for instructions. If your scope just has crosshairs, you can get a trajectory drop chart on the internet. Example, a .223(AR-15) will rise an inch and a half at 200 yards while a .308 stays flat. That's a considerable drop at a long distance! For example, a .308 zeroed at 100 yards will drop approximately twenty feet at 1,000 yards. The kit in front of the Site-In-Clean rifle rest is offered by few manufacturers that offer a bore-sighting kit. *Review: October 28, 2016*

Shooting
Class 2019

A few weeks ago, I gave a class on guns for six women. Some had a little shooting experience, but the majority had none or just fired a pistol or rifle several years ago. I think women must be in a position to protect themselves. I set up targets at ten yards, and we started with 22LR semi-automatic pistols, then 22 Magnums, next 380s, and finally 9mms. I believe the best home defense and concealed carry weapon is the one you can be proficient and comfortable with. If someone can put ten 22LR rounds in a target at ten yards but would be lucky to get one or two 9mm in the target and hates shooting the 9mm, the 22LR pistol or re-volver should be his or her weapon of choice. I think the ladies enjoyed the experience and hopefully, they will follow up with lessons and practice.

Review: July 13, 2019

Part of the Elderly Population

Since I am part of the elderly population, I use various aids that are helpful when I shoot rifles. When I was in the Army qualifying with my M1, I fired from the prone position, sitting position, and standing position. I am eighty-one years old now and it's too hard to get up from the prone and sitting position. I am not steady enough from the standing position.

I like the Caldwell shooter's table with a rifle barrel rest or a tripod. I have a site-in-clean accessory that is great for barrel sighting and rifle cleaning. View photos of my shooter's table on Ladies Day at the shooting range. Reversa Targets are excellent for shooting handguns and rifles. In my opinion, the top accessory for pistols and rifles are speed loaders. If you are loading a thirty-round magazine, the last eight or ten cartridges are torture. One of my favorite speed loaders is the Podavach. I can load a thirty round magazine for an AR-15 in about thirty seconds. *Review: December 18, 2021*

Ladies Shooting Class
September 20, 2020

Another exciting and fun day with lady shooters! My daughter, Donna, brought two of her friends from Indianapolis, and one local lady participated. They all did well and enjoyed themselves. One of the shooters who never fired a gun in her life, said she would never own a firearm. After shooting all day accurately, she told me that she was going to buy a pistol.

Closing out
Section IV

I have several cleaning kits and they all seem to work well. Most gun dealers have a preference, but I think that your choice will be correct.

My most expensive accessory is a Nikon P1000 camera. I purchased the P1000 because the telephoto is 125x magnification. I am posting a photo of steel at 200 yards.

Before I move on to Section V, there are some excellent suppliers online. I have dealt with Brownell's, Opticsplanet.com, and several other outstanding suppliers. I buy my ammo from bulkammo.com and under normal conditions, the price and service are excellent.

V

Firearm Manufacturers

This section is essential to some people, and others may skip this section. I want to know everything about the company and the product before I spend my money.

Several other great companies have excellent firearms—Sig-Sauer, CZ, Barrett, Wilson Combat, F&N, Bergara, just to name a few. Wikipedia and company sites have all the history and current information that will guide your purchases. YouTube reviews on guns, scopes, and accessories are excellent information sources. I did not want to write lengthy histories of the firearm companies because I don't know how interesting it would be to read in this book.

Browning
Arms Company

John Browning and his brother Matthew founded his company in 1878. I am listing some of Browning's most important designs that changed the firearm industry.

1. The 1911 and 45ACP ammunition: I think the 1911 is one of the most important guns in history. The military used it until 1986, and the popularity among civilian gun owners is extreme. My Wilson Combat 1911 is one of my favorite pistols.
2. The Browning Automatic Rifle: The BAR was manufactured late for World War I but was used extensively in World War II and the Korean Conflict.
3. The Winchester 1897 Shotgun: Winchester went from a crappy, heavy, lever-action shotgun to a Browning-designed pump shotgun.
4. There are several other great designs by John Browning in the M2 Machine Gun, the Auto Five Shotgun, and the Colt 380 Hammerless.

I didn't list the Browning High-Power because he did not finish the innovative pistol before he died.

I have several Browning firearms that I reviewed in the previous sections of this book. Browning Arms is a great quality firearm manufacturing company.

Colt's Manufacturing Company

Samuel Colt founded his manufacturing company in 1836. There were subsequent companies formed over the year and ownership changes. Colt has manufactured many famous firearms, including the Colt Walker, manufactured in 1847, the Colt Peacemaker, the Colt 1911, and the Colt Python. The 1911 is still in service with military and law enforcement worldwide.

Smith
& Wesson

Horace Smith and Dan Wesson founded the Smith & Wesson Company in 1852. Their objective was to develop the Volcanic Rifle and was renamed the Volcanic Repeating Arms in 1855. Oliver Winchester purchased the company in 1855 and retained Wesson for eight months as the plant manager.

Smith & Wesson reunited to form the Smith & Wesson Revolver Company. Through the years, the company evolved into a powerhouse manufacturer for revolvers, pistols, and rifles. They also have been in and out of financial trouble and through several ownership changes.

There is quite a lengthy history of the company available on the internet from Wikipedia and other sources.

Sturm,
Ruger & Company, Inc.

Sturm, Ruger & Co., Inc. is the largest firearm manufacturer in the United States. The company was founded in 1949 by Alexander McCormick Sturm and William Ruger.

Ruger dominates the 22LR Rimfire rifle and the 22LR Rimfire semiautomatic pistol market.

I own several Rugers, and every firearm, in my opinion, is good to excellent. My favorite Ruger revolver is the Super Redhawk 44 Magnum.

Henry
Repeating Arms

The Henry Repeating Arms was founded in 1996 by Louis Imperato and his son Anthony. They resurrected the old Henry Rifle and there is no lineage to Benjamin Tyler Henry, who invented and patented the first repeating rifle.

The company makes high-quality rifles and shotguns and is the leading manufacturer of lever-action rifles. The company's motto is "Made in America, Or Not Made At All." Henry's 22LR lever-action rifle sales are well over 1,000,000.

I own the Henry 22LR, 30-30, 357 Magnum, 44 Magnum, and the 308 Long Ranger. My next manufacturer is Winchester. The original Henry Rifle has a fascinating history that you can read about on Wikipedia and several other sites.

Winchester Repeating Arms Company

Oliver Winchester started as a clothing manufacturer in New Haven, Connecticut, and New York City. Winchester found out that Smith & Wesson were in financial trouble and acquired the Volcanic Repeating Arms Company with other investors. The company eventually became Winchester Repeating Arms Company and, with the help of Benjamin Tyler Henry, became profitable because of the Henry Rifle and the brass-cased .44 caliber cartridge.

Winchester manufactures high-quality firearms and has produced some of the most famous rifles in our country's history.

Remington
Arms Company

E. Remington founded the company in 1816 and was family owned until 1888. Remington manufactured excellent firearms and ammunition for years. The company was the largest manufacturer of rifles and shotguns and had military contracts.

Unfortunately, Remington filed for bankruptcy in 2020 and several companies purchased different divisions. Ruger is acquiring the property and assets of Marlin for $30.5 million. Vista Outdoor is spending $81.4 million for the Remington ammunition plant and the accessory business. They also will own the Remington name and trademarks. If anyone is interested, the story of the breakup of Remington is available on the internet.

Savage Arms

Arthur Savage founded his company in 1894 and manufactured quality firearms at excellent prices. Savage's ownership has changed several times over 126 years. During World War II, the Savage Company was heavily involved in the military production of firearms. Most of the Thompson submachine guns were manufactured by Savage and so was the Enfield bolt-action rifle for Britain.

Today Savage Arms manufactures quality, accurate rifles that have an excellent trigger known as the AccuTrigger. Savage Arms is a great company with a fascinating history. You can read about it online.

Glock

Glock is an Austrian company that manufactures polymer handguns that are known for their reliability. I have several Glocks but I am not a fan. I am listing, in my opinion, the pros and cons of a Glock.

Pros: The Glocks are-reliable, durable, light weight, easy to clean, and have an excellent magazine capacity.

Cons: It's an ugly pistol, has lousy sights, an average trigger, and a terrible ejection pattern. I usually get hit on my forehead once or twice out of a seventeen-round magazine.

Glock sells millions of pistols to law enforcement worldwide. I think there are better choices for concealed carry, home protection, and sport shooting. My opinion is definitely in the minority.

Heckler & Koch

Heckler & Koch was founded in 1949 by Edmund Heckler, Theodor Koch, and Alex Seidel. HK manufactures handguns, rifles, submachine guns, and grenade launchers. The company started as a military weapons manufacturing company, but in 1974, they diversified into law enforcement technology, hunting, and sport firearms. I own several HK weapons and they are excellent quality but are a little on the pricey side.

Beretta

Beretta is an Italian firearm manufacturing company that started its production in 1526. The company is the oldest firearm manufacturer globally and has acquired several gun manufacturing companies over the years. The parent company is Beretta Holdings, and it owns Beretta USA, Benelli, Franchi, Sako, Stoeger, Tikka, Uberti, and the Burris Optics Company.

Beretta is an industry giant and known for its high-quality products. Three of my favorite pistols are Berettas. Beretta is still a family-owned and managed company.

VI

Reviews
from
Friends

Ted Snedeker
Marshall, Illinois

I grew up with guns. On our farm in Southern Illinois, there were always rifles, shotguns, and pistols around. They were always loaded. My dad had two sayings about firearms, "An unloaded gun is no use to anyone" and "no one will ever be shot with an unloaded gun in my house."

From the time I was fourteen, I could tramp the woods and fields around our farm with Dad's Winchester model 62 terrorizing the squirrels and rabbits for miles around.

Through the years, I have owned dozens of various firearms, from a "sweet sixteen" Winchester autoloader to a .22 magnum "finger flick" lever gun by Marlin. My favorite shotgun was a model 101 Winchester over and under that I used to shoot skeet when I lived in Japan.

1911s

I became familiar with the 1911 when I was in the Navy, where I stood as a security guard in the sentry towers at the Nuclear Weapons Center Pacific on Coronado Island. The weapon we were issued was, of course, a government 1911. We were trained to use, clean, and care for it by Marine DIs at the Marine Corps firing range. Since we were using the 1911's on guard duty, we were authorized to go to the ordinance shack, draw a weapon and a couple of hundred rounds of ammo and practice with the .45s at their range whenever we had free time. Since I was a lowly seaman, my financial situation was thin to non-existent, so this "practice" became regular Saturday entertainment.

When I came back from Tokyo in 1970, I was assigned a job in a rough part of south Chicago. Thinking I might need a little protection, I traded the Marlin .22 mag for a 1911 that rode around under the driver's seat in various cars I owned for ten years.

The only time I needed it was when a hitchhiker threatened me, one I picked up on an all-night drive from San Angelo to home. Brandishing the weapon put a happy ending to the story and convinced the hitchhiker he shouldn't bring a knife to a gunfight.

In 1975, I got transferred to Alaska. My family and I lived there for four years. The company where I had my office was an electrical contracting firm that provided Union labor for my projects. We were modernizing the telephone network for the entire state. The owner, John Hollomon, was a bush pilot and big game hunter. He regaled me with tales of camping, hunting, and fishing in the Alaska bush all winter. He promised me trips to his cabin in the wilds of West Alaska as soon as the weather would permit. Since we had arrived on the first of January, I had a long winter to get prepared.

John informed me that West Alaska was bear country and that I should equip myself with a heavy handgun. Since I had owned a Ruger .22 mag single six at one time, I decided a .44 magnum Ruger was what I needed. I walked into a gun store, showed my Alaska driver's license, and walked out with a single action hand cannon. No background check, no silly wait time, just handed the man my credit card and exited stage left armed to the teeth. Did I mention, "I love Alaska?!"

Around the first of June, with a fishing trip laid out for the weekend, I went to the firing range in the foothills outside of Anchorage. I set up on the fifty-yard range and started blazing away at the bear-sized targets. After the first shot, I found holding on the target somewhat difficult. Anticipating the punishing recoil was not conducive to holding a steady sight picture. I was undoubtedly scaring the bear but doing him minor damage.

I moved to the twenty-five-yard targets and had the same result.

While I was busy scaring the targets, the Rangemaster walked up behind me and witnessed my woeful performance.

"You're not having much luck, are you?" he observed.

"No, I guess I need a lot more practice," I admitted.

"No, Son, what you need is different gear."

"Gear…?"

"Yes, get rid of that POS, Ruger. Get yourself a Smith in .41 magnum. They hit nearly as hard and are a lot easier on the shooter.… Just saying," he remarked and walked away.

The following week I showed up with model 57 hanging from my belt.

I passed the Rangemaster on the way to the firing platforms.

"I see you took my advice," he said, looking down at the Smith. "Can I give you one bit more?"

"Sure," I answered, wondering, "what now?"

"Get rid of that belt holster, get a shoulder rig that carries that hand cannon under your left arm."

"Hmm, shoulder holster?" I mumbled, thinking that shoulder holsters were mostly for police and detectives.

"Yes, out in the bush, you will always have on a vest, and you will be crawling into and out of planes, boats, and other conveyances. If you have a gun hanging from your belt, it will get hung up, and you are liable to lose your gun right when you need it most."

The crusty old Rangemaster was right on all counts; after a couple of trips to the range with the Smith, I could put all six rounds in a teacup at twenty-five yards, and the shoulder rig was perfect.

I got into hunting in a big way in Alaska. I ended up with a collection of Sako rifles in .338, 7mm magnum, and 30.06, all with Leopold gold ring glass. I hand loaded and hunted and fished all over Alaska.

I have few regrets in my life, but leaving Alaska is one.

After I came out of Alaska, I reluctantly disposed of all my guns but the .41 Smith. I just couldn't bear to part with it, and I still planned on returning to Alaska for camping and fishing trips.

In 1984, we were living in Indianapolis in a home on Westfield Boulevard, right on the canal. I came home from a full week trip camping on a wilderness lake with John Hollomon, where we slaughtered the pike and muskie. It was a great trip!

It was late when Kay picked me up at the Indianapolis airport. I was bushed. As a result, I just set my pack at the end of the bed, dove into the shower, and crashed.

About two in the morning, I was awakened by what sounded like glass breaking. After a few moments, I turned over to go back to sleep, thinking it was just a bump in the night. A couple of seconds later, I heard a distinct crash. It was glass-breaking! I realized someone was trying to break into the house.

I rolled over and slid the nightstand drawer open where I kept the Smith. It wasn't there!

As I struggled to come awake, listening to various noises coming up the steps, I realized my .41 was still in my pack where it had come home as check luggage. I rolled out of bed, pulled on a robe, and dug the pistol out of the pack. Then I had to find the ammo, which was in another pouch pocket on the pack. By the time I got it loaded and set off to confront the situation downstairs, Kay had awakened as well.

I told her I wasn't sure what was going on, but I was going to investigate. I told her to stay in our room. Of course, she didn't. She came down the steps right behind me.

I paused at the bottom of the steps to look through the dining room and see the kitchen door. There was a hand coming through the broken glass, trying to get the knob open. It was an older house, and the latch was stubborn, so the miscreant was having a bit of difficulty.

Kay walked by me down the hall and stood looking into the kitchen.

"There's been an explosion!" She shouted. "There is glass all over the floor!" She was still half asleep and missed seeing the hand coming through the door.

"Ah, she is visible in the hall light. Whoever is trying to get in will see her and split," I thought to myself.

Wrong. The intruder just kept trying to come through the door.

That angered me. If I hadn't been there, the thug would have come on in the house. But I was there.

I slipped along the dining room wall and slid over to the door out of the hall light in a shadow. I reached down and pulled the door open. I was confronted by a muscular young man, blonde and shirtless. He was standing on the driveway, putting his head about belt high to where I was standing.

I put the .41 right in his face.

"Down on the concrete!" I ordered.

"NO!" he shouted, backing away.

Now, in retrospect, I am sure he was saying, "NO, don't shoot me."

But in my adrenaline-fueled fog, I heard, "NO, I'm not getting down!"

"KABOOM!" I pulled off an inch or two and squeezed off a round less than three inches from his right ear. The muzzle blast knocked him down.

Kay called the police, and they must have been less than a block away because they pulled into the drive almost immediately. The responding officer walked up, sized up the situation, and rolled the would-be home invader over on his back. He shook his head and looked up at me.

"Oh, Sir, why didn't you shoot him?"

It turned out there were two of them. The officer sent his partner down the alley in pursuit, and he returned shortly with an accomplice. It turned out the pair's leader was out on parole and was running a fencing operation where the police were planning on raiding and arresting him in the next couple of days. I did not even have to go to testify. They just locked him back up.

I am retired now and living on a farm in Southern Illinois near where I grew up. The crime rate here is minimal to nonexistent, but I still keep a bedside piece. My current home defender is a bit more modern.

BUL M5

The BUL is a polymer frame 1911 clone with a double-stack magazine that I keep loaded with fifteen rounds. I like the pistol for its lightweight, firm feel and tight groups. I like it in the 1911 format because I don't have to think about using it. I keep it beside my bed with a round chambered, safety off but hammer down. All I must do is pick it up, pull the hammer back and shoot.

Indiana Shooter
and Collector

I am very grateful to a friend of mine for inviting me to his home so I could look at his gun collection. Due to the size and value of his collection, I will protect his anonymity. His name in this publication is Indiana Shooter and Collector. I was overwhelmed by the custom and rare guns. The Shooter has four custom rifles that reach out accurately to 1,000 yards. The barrels and suppressors are one unit. I looked at a photo of a three-shot group at 1,000 yards that would fit in a quarter. I am going to post several images. They all have a story, but I was so busy admiring his collection that I didn't write notes. One of the most exciting guns, in my opinion, was his 1894 Parker 12- gauge shotgun.

The Browning safe door is the entrance to Shooter's Gun Room. All of the Shooter's firearms have a story. I

think if I spent forty hours with him and his weapons, I would write a minimum of seventy-five pages and have at least two hundred photos.

The customized bench rifle, below, weighs thirty-two pounds and is a 1,000 yard gun.

The custom-made Gatling gun, below left, was made by the Shooter using Ruger 10/22 rifles. A pair of Colt Pythons, never fired are below right. At the bottom are two single action Colt Revolvers.

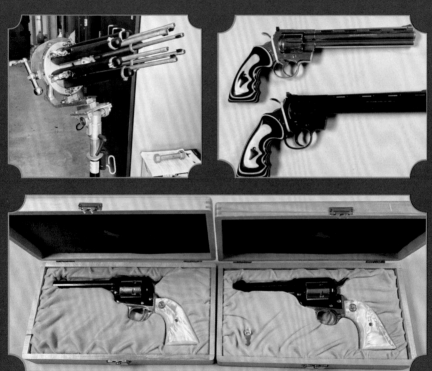

I believe the photo above is a 1964 Browning. Below are more guns in the shooter's collection.

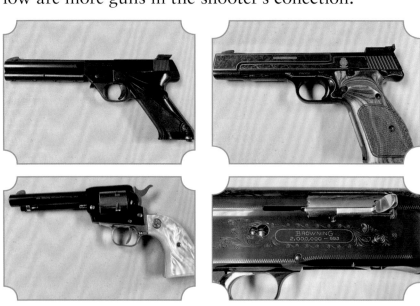

Jay Fledderman
Batesville, Indiana

My favorite firearm is a model 1894 Winchester 30-30 lever action with octagon barrel, manufactured in 1918.

The Winchester was one of my dad's guns I probably fired this gun way more than dad ever did because when I was younger, I was always getting it out of his gun cabinet when he was not home and shooting it.

It is in good shape and is pretty accurate at 100 yards with open sights. Coyotes didn't stand a chance.

Of course, it is special to me because it was dad's, and second, that is one of the best-made rifles I have ever seen.

***

Dale Enneking
Batesville, Indiana

A friend of mine, Dale Enneking, allowed me to borrow his Colt Anaconda 44 Magnum to shoot and review.

His review of his classic revolver was short and sweet. He thinks the trigger, balance, sights, and accuracy are excellent. My review coincides with his with a few exceptions.

I was comparing the Anaconda to my Ruger Super Redhawk. I like the Anaconda better, except the Redhawk's grips are wider and a more excellent fit. The gun is well made but not the same quality as a Colt Python. Testing the Anaconda was an absolute pleasure! I was target shooting from twenty-five to thirty feet. During my first six rounds, I fired double-action while moving, and I was pointing and shooting. The photo of my target will show the six rounds to the left. The rest of my shooting was stationary, rapid-fire single action. The 44 Magnum is so accurate that I think if I had paused a few seconds before each shot, I would have destroyed the bullseye. I like the gun, but due to the insane prices, I will probably never own one. Hickok45 has an excellent video on YouTube on the Anaconda and the old and new Python.

My Brother, Ron Reidy
Loveland, Colorado

A Ninety-One-Year-Old Can Still Shoot

My brother Ron will be ninety-two years old in December, and he still loads his ammo and goes to the range when he is not dealing with health issues. Ron was shooting large targets with a Remington 700ADL chambered in 308 Win at 100 yards when he was eighty-eight years old. About five months ago, at twenty-five yards with a Rossi M92 44 magnum, he was hitting the bullseye twenty out of twenty shots. I will be eighty in January, and if I am alive at his age, I hope I have all my mental and physical faculties to hit small steel plates still. *Review: August 22, 2018*

Ron died earlier this year at age ninety-three. He was a World War II veteran and part of the greatest generation.

Brad Mehlon
Batesville, Indiana

I am posting a CZ 75 review from Brad Mehlon. I have not fired a CZ 75 or any CZ pistol, so I researched the CZ 75. Every review that I read or watched on You-Tube was very positive. I hope that I can talk Brad into allowing me to shoot his CZ 75 this spring. I posted a Hickok45 review on the CZ.

Edited: December 8, 2020

The CZ 75 SP-01 9mm is an all-steel, full-size pistol with a 4.7" barrel. The SP-01 carries an unloaded weight of around thirty-nine ounces, 1913 accessory rail, and "true dot" night sights. The CZ comes with two 18 round high-capacity magazines. The SP-01 is a single/double action pistol with ambidextrous safety.

For anyone searching for a 9mm pistol, the SP-01 would be an excellent example of one with modest recoil, supreme accuracy, and unmatched ergonomics. It's a beautiful gun and a joy to shoot. If you are like me, you will have a hard time putting this pistol down.

Review: December 11, 2016

Eric Blanken
Batesville, Indiana

I recently had the pleasure of shooting an FN PS90. Eric from Batesville allowed me to shoot and review his PS90. Eric has an unusual rifle, and it's not cheap. MSRP is $1499.00 without a red dot optic. Once we got the optic zeroed at twenty-five yards, it was very accurate and fun to shoot. After we finished shooting the FN, I did some research and watched some videos on YouTube. The muzzle velocity is 2034 feet per second, which is almost twice the speed of sound. The ammo was 40-grain V-max manufactured by Hornady for FN. We did not shoot beyond twenty-five yards, but it shoots flat, and I think it will be on the money at fifty yards with a slight drop at 100 yards. The distance from the optic to the barrel is about five inches, so if you are zeroed at twenty-five yards and decide that you want to shoot at twenty-five feet, you will have to shoot over the top of the target. Very easy takedown for cleaning. But the ammo is expensive. The best price that I found was $1120.00 for 2,000 rounds. Fifty-six cents per round is more than I pay for 308Win. There are some excellent videos on YouTube for this Bullpup rifle.

Eric likes the fifty-round magazine, size, trigger, and the red-dot scope once we zeroed it at twenty-five yards. He also wanted the easy loading and the ejection from the bottom of this unique firearm.

Review: May 2, 2019

Jeremiah Volk
Greensburg, Indiana

The gun above is a Ruger Super Blackhawk. I've been able to shoot this firearm on numerous occasions with my dad. This gun is a very reliable gun to own. I've experienced zero issues or errors while shooting it. Due to the great experience I've had while using it, I would rate it at 100% reliability. The gun feels very comfortable while holding and handling. The balance while handling the firearm is good but not great. While shooting, however, I have noticed numerous times that the accuracy is not the best. I believe the inaccuracy is due to the barrel being shorter. Even with the short barrel and poor accuracy, the Ruger is a quality revolver. I would recommend this firearm for anyone looking for a decent handgun at the end of the day.

Review: September 29, 2020

Bob Prophater
Sugar Grove, Ohio

I purchased the M & P Shield 2.0 9mm to carry it daily. I tried several other 9mms and based upon how the Shield fit my hand along with it being accurate and affordable, all played equal parts in my choosing the Shield.

I won't waste time on the specs as they are available online.

I do like the white dots sights; two at the rear and one at the front.

As I said, the Shield fits my hand for comfort, balance, and grip.

The clip ejects and not just releases.

My Shield came with safety, which I wanted as I have a round in the chamber at all times.

After firing the first fifty rounds and adjusted to the trigger pull, I consistently shot a 5" grouping at fifteen to twenty feet. I have put well over a couple of thousand rounds through it and never encountered any problems.

Many will prefer the Glock or other brands, but this was the best match for my hand and need.

I have also opted instead of an inside or outside the waistband to use a Sneaky Pete holster. I have been carrying for over three years now, and no one has questioned me on this. *Review: October 2, 2020*

Scott Bollinger
Cincinnati, Ohio

My name is Scott Bollinger. I am from Cincinnati, Ohio, and as a child growing up, I never had any experience with firearms. At eighteen years old, I thought it would be a good idea to join the U.S. Army Military Police Corps. For the next four years, I developed an appreciation and respect for all kinds of weapons, pistols, and rifles. So, when Ohio passed the law to carry concealed handguns in 2005, I felt I had earned the right to apply for one. With my clean record and the training that I received, I was approved. So, it was then time to purchase a concealed carry firearm.

I already owned a few guns, but I looked for something more concealable and with an excellent name and reputation. I like to buy American, so I started looking at Ruger and Smith & Wesson. I like the looks and feel of the Ruger SR9C. The slide is steel, but the grip is plastic, giving it reduced weight but durable performance. It has an adjustable rear sight to help zero it in. It also has a rail on the front if you want to mount a laser. It has a mechanical safety, which is very important to me to prevent accidental discharge while removing from a holster. There is no hammer on the back to get hung up in clothing should I have to deploy it in an emergency. It came with two magazines, a 10 round, and a seventeen round. The ten rounder has a spacer on it to make it slightly longer for hand as you are holding it. I prefer the seventeen rounder as I am carrying it concealed. I like to have more rounds if I need them. The overall length difference is about 3/4" because of the smaller magazine spacer. The pistol is amazingly comfortable to fire at the range. It pops in your hand as expected but is well balanced. I have fired maybe 800-1000 rounds through it without a single misfire, magazine problem, or shell discharge. I bought it in 2011 for $525 from a dealer. I am not a large person, and the soft edges make it pretty easy to conceal. I purchased a 9mm because the ammo is pretty reasonably priced and readily available for purchase. I use Hornady Critical Defense ammo while carrying.

Jake Baumer
Batesville, Indiana

This review will be on one of my favorite guns, often overlooked by many people. Let's just say if the world turned to complete hell and you could only have one firearm, what would you pick? Easy for me. Remington 870. I received my first 870 in 20 gauge around Christmas, 2003, at eleven. A few years went by where I needed to gain a few pounds to handle Dad's 12. These Remington 870s are about

as American as apple pie, and it ranks right behind a 1911. It is easily customizable, basically "the small block Chevy of firearms," and the reliability is second to none.

Any shell, load, buried in the mud or kicked off a mountain, it's going to shoot and light up the intended target. It can handle most North American game. At short range, you're bringing home supper. These 870s are not flashy by any means, and they certainly let you know you're behind one as the recoil is compared to semiautomatic shotguns. It's a banger. In 2020, as crazy as the gun market has gone, $350–$400ish, will bring one of these shotguns home, so it's a pretty affordable price point for a well-made gun, a gun that all Americans need in their arsenal. Bring it back twenty years ago, and every deer hunter in Indiana headed to the woods mid-November with one.

Last but not least, absolutely nothing scares a home intruder more than the click-clack of racking an 870. If not, then whatever is in your home isn't a human. I hope all readers enjoyed this review. Hopefully, this brings back the interest in that 870 sitting in the back of the gun safe as it is one of the most underrated and finest firearms in America. *Review: October 7, 2020*

Kevin Brogan
Dublin, Ohio

The Taurus Judge. It's great for home defense and not bulky like a shotgun. I have three 410 rounds in it and two 45 Colt rounds in it. 410 rounds have stopping power, and the 45 rounds will finish him or her off if they keep coming. I have others, but this is the most convenient one for an initial threat in the middle of the night!

Greg Niese
Batesville, Indiana

I'm a life-long shooter, U.S. Army trained, current FFL custom firearms dealer, Barrett Rec7 DI .223/5.56.

I got into the AR scene about eight years ago, after spending all my time with bolt action and semi-auto rifles along with a lot of Knight and Thompson Center Muzzleloaders. I was impressed with the AR platform and the Mil-Spec capabilities. In 2012, I purchased a DPMS carbine in .223/5.56 and started upgrading and shooting. I also bought a DPMS AR10 in .308. Both were reliable and fun to shoot, so I spent many nights and weekends blowing up Tannerite. My neighbors were impressed.

I wanted to upgrade and knew my next choice was a Rock River Arms, so I bought an RRA Operator. It's incredibly accurate. I wore the barrel out over time and so I re-barreled it with an RRA stainless barrel from the factory.

I decided after hunting with it for a while that the gun is too heavy. So, I started researching for my replacement that would last me a decade or more. I narrowed it down to Barrett. I considered a custom build, but then there's the mismatch of parts and maybe not being as reliable as one fresh out of the factory.

Barrett, all USA made in Murfreesboro, Tennessee, uses all quality parts. It's one of the nicest ARs I've ever handled.

It has all Magpul hardware which is the best you're going to find.

Reliability in the short time I've been shooting it, I've been impressed with its abilities.

Accuracy right out of the case with open sights at fifty yards (best for my old eyes), I was hitting dead on.

I am mounting a scope very soon to open it up and get some range.

The trigger is an ALG QMS trigger, which is smooth and has a tight release.

The sights are Magpul fully adjustable flip-up rear peep and flip up the front pin.

The build quality is second to none, and as tight as any machined part.

Recommendation for purchasing the firearm. I would repurchase it. Great price, excellent quality!

Review: October 8, 2020

Chaz Kaiser
Batesville, Indiana

I have several guns, but I want to review my Tavor and Walther because I use both in the 2 Gun Competition. I will write about the competition later. My Tavor is manufactured in Israel and is a Bullpup rifle, a more compact AR-15. The Tavor is used by Israel Military and law enforcement and by several other countries. I have a 1x6x24 illuminated scope on the Bullpup, and it is excellent. Several people asked why I like the Tavor over a conventional AR-15, and the reason is simple. In a self-defense situation in close quarters, I have firepower and maneuverability.

The finish on the Bullpup is excellent, the Geissele trigger is outstanding, the accuracy is perfect, and the value is just so good. I highly recommend this firearm.

My Walther P99 is no longer available, but I hope that I never have to replace it. The Walther's finish, trigger, accuracy, and value are excellent.

My buddy, Walt Enneking, and I started the Tactical Shooters Alliance at Coon Hunter's in Batesville four years ago.

The Tactical Shooters Alliance is an organization that offers monthly defensive two-gun matches to the affiliate gun clubs. Each club completes the exact match under the official TSA rules and guidelines. Those match results are sent to TSA headquarters, where members of the TSA can view them and see not only how they finished against others competing at their club but how they finished against every other TSA member in the nation! This model offers TSA members the opportunity to be ranked nationally and the chance to accurately gauge their ability and physically see in the match results data where they can improve and where they are performing well. If you've been looking for something new in the shooting sports world, the Tactical Shooters Alliance has a lot to offer you and your local gun club. *Review: October 9, 2020*

Nathan Johnson
Marysville, Ohio

Many are no stranger to the 1911, which Browning designed over 100 years ago. It's incredible to see its design stay so popular today, even after many years of other options.

I was always attracted to the 1911. And hence, why I chose to select one for review after Mr. Reidy reached out. I am reviewing a pistol, which I carry most everyday; however, I will do my best to offer a non-biased review and offer the pros/cons of one of my favorite firearms.

The Kimber Ultra CDP (Custom Defense Package) is a 3" 1911 designed with quality and concealed carry in mind. I have other options in the household, but this usually is my go-to for concealment. Here's why: Kimber nailed it when they offered the 1911 in a 3" barrel, designed as a defensive sidearm. At first glance, one can easily see the rounded lines, serrations, checkering in all the right places, and even ambidextrous thumb safety, all engineered with a carry-minded person in mind.

The CDP is one of Kimber's highest line of their 1911 lines. It comes at a premium of roughly 500 dollars more than their average 1911s, but for a good reason. This firearm has a stainless slide, an aluminum frame, a short, crisp, and predictable trigger. It has upgraded, including night sights, ambidextrous thumb safety, backstrap, trigger guard, and even underneath checking. Kimber left no stone unturned when designing this package.

I have run roughly 4k rounds of all types of 45 ACP through this sidearm for functionality. It's not an exaggeration that this pistol will eat any brand, grain, reload, or factory type of ammo. A remarkable fact knowing how steep a feed ramp is on a 3" 1911 is one reason I choose to carry this particular model.

As for some cons, I've owned and carried this pistol for almost eight years. To say I've gotten to know it well is an understatement. With that said, here are some of its downsides as I compare it to my other carry pistols. Capacity is probably its biggest problem. Although expected for 1911, the Ultra CDP only has a 7+1 capacity. Many would argue, including me, that the accuracy and familiarity of use with such a fine gun is a better trade-off. That's what I've decided and is why I practice magazines reloading at the range.

Another thing to note is the aluminum frame. However a beautiful firearm, the black paint coating on the aluminum frame will show some wear after a while. I can't argue or complain too much, especially knowing that I've carried this for eight years, but it's still a negative knowing how much the gun costs.

In a nutshell, I recommend the Kimber CDP line to any 1911 lover. Although not cheap, they are roughly half the price of total custom 1911s. In comparison to an Ed Brown or comparable, you will still get the feel of a very smooth yet tight tolerance 1911 for less money. The CDP line comes in 3", 4", and 5" barrel lengths. I own all and can honestly say they are among some of my favorite 1911s that I own. *Review: October 9, 2020*

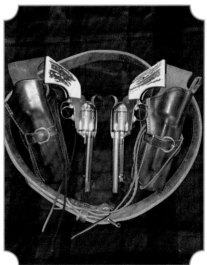

Phil Hadley
Greensburg, Indiana

I own several firearms, and one of my favorite revolvers is the Ruger Vaquero. I have two chambered in

Colt 45LC. I opted for the 45LC cartridge for several reasons. 1) I think that if you have the original Old West Single-Action Look, the Old West Cartridge is appropriate. 2) Excellent stopping power. 3) The 45LC was developed in the 1870s for the Single-Action Colt Army Revolver.

I modified the Vaqueros by installing hammer springs, Corian Stag grips, and a trigger job. My Ruger is a fun gun to shoot, the stock sights are excellent, and the accuracy is acceptable. If you want a feel of the Old West and enjoy shooting for fun, I highly recommend this great revolver. *Review: October 16, 2020*

Jim Doyle
Batesville, Indiana

My name is Jim Doyle, a long-time gun enthusiast, and part-time shooter. When Larry asked me to review the AK47, I was hesitant because I am not a writer nor a historian. I will not include all the specifications of the AK. You can find accurate specs on Google or Wikipedia. My best recollection is that I purchased my Saiga back in the early 2000s. It is a Saiga, Legion Izhevsk Russia, & Arsenal Las Vegas NV. The cartridge is 762x39. It is a Russian-made Saiga. That is how it was explained to me when I purchased the gun. I have made no modifications to this rifle. Again, all this technical info is available on Google or Arsenals' website.

My overall impression of this gun is excellent for multiple reasons. Historically, it is very reliable, almost indestructible under normal to adverse conditions. The weather has not been an issue for me. The colossal safety is ideal for gloves as you simply slap it down to fire. I have never had a "jam" when feeding, and I have used some very old Russian ammunition. As far as accuracy goes, I would never blame the gun. I have fired this only to about 100 yards and was on paper. For me, that's acceptable. The weapon has metal battle sites—adjustable front and adjustable rear as you move the rear sight forward using the ramp. Supposedly it's adjustable from 100–900 meters, but from research, it is not a long-range sight system. Again, there are plenty of ballistics books to be found. The trigger system is not a finesse system. It is a firing platform. You will not confuse this trigger with a custom trigger job, but it gets the job done. There is no play in my particular trigger. The build quality is outstanding in my estimation. My AK is stamped metal, so again, this is not a Wilson Arms quality-build.

I had read that some AKs were milled but not confident where or when they began some milled parts at some point in time. It is a mass-produced weapon. I have had no issue/failures with this gun, but it also is not heavily used. It is a black polymer rifle that shows no signs of wear after about twenty years of misuse and neglect. The AK is not a fancy firearm, but this weapon's reliability and longevity make it an excellent addition for a gun collection or a home defense weapon. (But it is not supposed to be.) It is a mass-produced, stamped, very reliable, inexpensive rifle that supplies armies, worldwide Rebel groups, sport shooters, and personal defense use. Hell, Rambo has used them. My gun is all stock and factory equipped. There are ample ways to modify this gun in any way you want.

I paid approximately $450.00 several years ago, and I would repurchase it. Keeping in mind the gun's use for me is pleasure shooting vs. long-range accuracy: dependability vs. show firearm. In my opinion, this is a blunt weapon vs. surgical precision. I'm sure this will draw plenty of criticism. It is just one opinion. Again, this is more of a straightforward review vs. surgical— only one user's view. Google is your friend for all the technical information. I didn't make my living using this gun. I never depended on it in any threatening situation. My AK was and is just for fun, and I take this review as such. Information is from memory, and accuracy is not guaranteed. *Review: October 20, 2020*

Walt Enneking
Napoleon, Indiana

Shooting has been a big part of my life since I was a kid. I've devoted a large portion of my life to learning and teaching others about firearms, with my primary focus being on firearms safety and defensive employment. On the subject, I've built a healthy resume. In 2004, I enlisted in the United States Marine Corps to become a machine gunner assigned to Anti-Terrorism Battalion under the 2nd Marine Division. Anti-Terrorism Battalion was formed right after 9/11 as a specialized unit for detecting, deterring, and defending against terrorist operations worldwide. I deployed with AT in 2005–2006 to Ashraf, Iraq and again for thirteen months from 2007–2008 to Al Anbar province, Iraq provided personal security detail for the commanding generals of Iraq, high-level government officials, foreign dignitaries, and other VIPs, including Chuck Norris (although it's not clear who was protecting who on that one). I was certified by Blackwater Training Center in 2006 in High-Risk Executive Protection and Advanced Evasive driving. In 2008 I decided to exit the Marine Corps and come home for everyday life. Once home, I became an NRA certified instructor and started a business named Iron Sight Tactical. I provided instruction to the general public on the safe and defensive use of handguns and long guns. I also co-founded a small organization called the Tactical Shooters Alliance. We host monthly tactical 2-Gun competitions using scenario-based stages and re-al-world tactics. While I don't teach anymore because of time constraints, shooting will always be a staple in my life.

When Larry asked me to review my favorite firearm, I had a hard time deciding. I've had the good fortune to work with many fantastic weapons systems over the years. After the Marine Corps, I began participating in the International Defensive Pistol Association, where I ran a Springfield Armory Xd45 and Xd9.

After ten years of shooting the Xd platform, I wanted to try something new, so I moved to the Smith & Wesson M&P series. I loved the ergonomics of the M&P but found it had some trouble with consistent accuracy, so again I was on the hunt for a new pistol.

While at the Indianapolis 1500-gun show promot-ing the Tactical Shooters Alliance, I visited booth after booth searching for a little more competition-oriented weapon, but I was also on a budget. Enter the Canik TP9 SFX. I had no working knowledge of Canik. My first impressions of the Canik were excellent. It doesn't get a lot of praise for its appearance, but the two-tone finish and ported slide appealed to me. It looked like something John Wick may have under his suit jacket, and that's good enough for me. The ergonomics were impressive. It has front and rear serrations machined into the slide, and three different options included for the back strap, it feels great in hand. One of my big gripes about other handguns I've shot were access to the slide latch release and magazine release. I liked the design of the slide latch release on this model. With ample real estate and protrusion, it allowed for easy release but didn't stick out so much that it may accidentally be held down while firing, keeping it from going to slide lock on the last round. This problem I've encountered on many other frames. The magazine release is extended from the factory and comes with three different options to suit you. The trigger on this weapon is what impressed me the most. Most polymer-framed defensive pistols come with a trigger that leaves a lot to be desired; heavy and mushy breaks with long resets are common, so many shooters upgrade their triggers with companies like Apex. That's not the case here. Canik designed this pistol from the ground up for the budget-minded competitive shooter. The trigger break is crisp and light, with an excellent reset for those clean hammered pairs. It's also worth mentioning that the TP9 SFX comes optics ready out of the box with mounting plates for every popular pistol optic included if that's your cup of tea.

So, all looks good, right? I'd only heard the name Canik, and like most things obscure in the firearms world, if it's not popular, there's usually a reason. So off to YouTube, I went to get my learn on. I had no clue how this weapon would perform or if it would even be reliable. The info I found on YouTube solidified my decision. One reviewer had about 2000 rounds through his Canik with not one jam or malfunction. The Canik TP9 SFX passed muster, and at an MSRP of $550 and a sale price of $480, I had a hard time passing it by.

Time to get this gun on the range. At initial inspection, this weapon felt front heavy due to the 5.2 inch long barrel, but once I had a loaded mag in, it balanced out beautifully. Firing the first shots, I paid special attention to how this weapon recoiled and how much noticeable muzzle rise there was. Not a factor here. This gun runs on a rail, but you have to give it a solid platform to operate like all handguns. Proper grip and stance are essential.

I have found all firearms have different break-in periods before achieving optimal accuracy. For example, most AR-15 rifles need about 200 rounds through them before they start becoming consistent in the accuracy department. With the Canik, I've noticed the accuracy has only improved, probably due to breaking it in and my improved relationship with my new gun. My first shots did not disappoint, though. I never did bench it to find out exactly how good it is, but from standing at fifteen yards, I could hold four inch groups. After more trigger time, that group has improved. This weapon is capable of hanging with guns three times its value as far as accuracy goes. Hitting a steel popper at fifty yards is well within the performance of this gun.

One thing to be noted on accuracy is that while the barrel seems to be quality, the Warren sights that come with it are just ok. Primarily my complaint is with the front sight. It could stand to be a little wider as it tends to float in the rear sight aperture.

My second complaint is with the trigger safety. I've found it to be a little crude and tends to hang up unless you have your trigger finger in just the right spot upon pull, causing it to catch and throw a shot. I have adapted to this problem, but I haven't ruled out modifying it.

I have only about 600 rounds through the Canik TP9 SFX with zero stoppages or malfunctions as I write this. I make it a point not to clean a new firearm until it fails. So far, the Canik TP9 SFX has delivered as advertised. My TP9 is an out-of-the-box competition-ready weapon that has surpassed all of my expectations. If you are looking for a budget weapon in the competition genre, don't pass up the Canik TP9 SFX.

Review: October 27, 2020

Tony Schantz
Batesville, Indiana

Tony Schantz is sporting the iconic Henry Rifle Model 1862. The Rifle is a lever-action tubular magazine Rifle and the iconic Winchester lever-action rifle that helped tame the Wild American West. The original was a .44 caliber Rimfire, but the model Tony has is .44-40. Some Union Soldiers used the rifle in the Civil War who carried it with pride. The rifle has an exceptionally high fire rate for the period, but tactics had not advanced to the point to take advantage, so scouts and raiding parties primarily used them. Some of the rifles found their way west and were used by the Sioux and Cheyenne to obliterate General Custer and his men at Little Big Horn's battle. The rifles were initially manufactured by the New Haven Arms Company, which later evolved into the great Winchester Repeating Arms Company. *Review: November 2, 2020*

Bill Kotz
Osgood, Indiana

My favorite concealed carry firearm is the Smith & Wesson J frame 38 Special AIRLITE TI model 342 pre-lock. IT'S NOT A MODEL 642 "AIR WEIGHT!" This pocket gun weighs only 11.3 ounces and is barely noticeable when carried in a pocket. Many times, I have to check to make sure I'm carrying it. The frame is of scandium alloy construction, while the cylinder is made of titanium to stand up to the +P ammo pressure. The outer barrel is scandium with a steel inner barrel. This S&W hammerless weapon comes in double action only and has been carefully finished with no sharp edges or angles to snag on clothing, ensuring a quick draw should the need arise. It slips in and out of my pocket effortlessly. It fires 38 Special +P jacketed ammo.

The jacketed ammo recoil could cause lead bullets to come loose from their case and jam the cylinder. The recoil is noticeable due to the lightweight and 1 7/8 inches barrel, but it's manageable. I was able to score groups from 1 1/2 to 2 1/2 inches at fifteen yards after some practice using my Crimson Trace laser sight. I was able to put all five shots into a softball-sized group center mass on a human silhouette target at twenty feet while firing rapidly. HR FUNK states this S&W model 342 is his favorite CC weapon. There's an excellent review on YouTube by HR FUNK on the S&W 342 TI. It's worth watching! *Review: November 4, 2020*

Brayton Deal
Batesville, Indiana

I own several firearms, and my favorite is a Remington 700 with a Bushnell 3x9x40 Scope. My 700 is an easy rifle to like. I am listing the attributes of this excellent gun below.

1. Easy to shoot.
2. Inexpensive ammunition during regular times.

3. Exceptional durability.
4. Great value.
5. Terrific grouping at 100 and 200 yards.
6. Smooth bolt-action.
7. Reliable; no misfires.
8. It feels like it was custom-made for me. It's a great fit.
9. Easy to clean.
10. Manufactured in the USA.

My only dislike is it's a heavy hunting rifle.

Review: November 4, 2020

Bob Weiler
Batesville, Indiana

The handgun is a Rock Island Armory TAC Ultra FS 10mm in a 1911 platform.

I had always wanted a 1911, and when the 10mm round became a legal caliber to deer hunt, I decided to purchase one as a sidearm while hunting. What I didn't realize at the time was how much I would enjoy shooting it. It is exceptionally smooth and accurate, and the recoil is minimal and allows for keeping the gun on target while firing successive rounds.

The RIA TAC Ultra FS 10mm is a full framed weapon with an eight round magazine. The slide is smooth and tight when racked. It has very aggressive grips making it ideal if wearing tactical gloves. It also has a high shoulder which fits my large hands rather well. I like the adjustable rear dot sights, but I don't care much for the orange fiber optic front sight. I don't feel it catches the light very well and can be hard to find when trying to pull up on a target. The front sight is something I plan to upgrade in the future. The trigger has minimal take-up and breaks around five pounds. It has the classic "cock and lock" of all 1911s with ambidextrous safeties, along with additional safety in the back of the grip where the crease of your palm would sit. One of the things I like about the weapon is how "tight" everything is. It gives a feel of quality when everything moves smoothly and locks in place tightly.

In summary, the RIA TAC Ultra FS has a slightly surprising feel of quality and incredible accuracy for the price. It is an excellent weapon for target shooting, hunting, or defense. It is a little cumbersome and heavy for my liking in concealed carry, but I typically carry inside the waistband and is probably typical for a full-frame weapon. When carrying outside the waistband while hunting, it is barely noticeable. If you are a 1911 fan, I highly recommend adding this weapon to your collection. *Review: November 5, 2020*

Kentucky
Gun Collector

I had the privilege of going to Kentucky Gun Collector's home to write a review on some of his firearms. I did a terrible job because I was overwhelmed and out of my league. I was like a little kid in a candy store. His collection is magnificent, and he has a story about all of his guns. His recall is impeccable, and his collection, in my opinion, is priceless. The Colt Snake gun collection is mind-boggling. I would guess that he has around fifty original Colt Pythons, and most of them are unfired. I honestly believe that every firearm that he has is museum quality. Two of his rifles manufactured by Savage Arms for the Dodge brothers in the early 1900s are two of a kind. A Gold Savage 32 caliber manufactured from 1904 to 1908 with the serial number "1." Captain Jack's photo and the previous image with

an envelope behind the rifle he used in the Buffalo Bill Wild West Show posted some pictures. If I have a second printing, I will ask the collector for another interview with pictures of his top ten guns. The collector wants his anonymity for safety reasons. I am so fortunate to be one of a select few that has seen his collection.

Michael Spreckelson
Greensburg, Indiana

My Winchester Model 61 is an excellent small game rifle. I grew up hunting with a Winchester Model 62A, but the 61 is sleeker and allows an optic without modifying the gun. I love the pump action design. It is comfortable to shoot and carry in the woods. These rifles were used years ago in shooting galleries. They are incredibly accurate and dependable. I love shooting mine whenever I have a chance. I have two model 61s, one chambered in 22 Short, 22, and 22LR. My other Winchester chambered in 22 Magnum is a joy to shoot, but I tend to use the 61 22LR more often.

Addendum

I want to thank everyone who purchased my book, and I hope you enjoyed reading the reviews as much as I enjoyed writing them. My sincere thanks to my friends for taking the time out of their busy lives to write a review. Please refer your friends to my website larryreidy.net to purchase books or orangefrazer.com, Amazon.com, and Amazon Kindle.

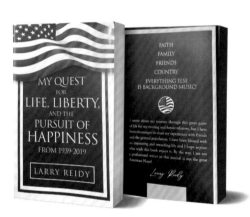

My previous book was a condensed autobiography that I wrote for my children, grandchildren, great-grand-children, and future generations. I originally planned to write a 500 page book, but I thought 250 to 300 should be the maximum so that the grandchildren would read it. A friend of mine, Ted Snedeker, who is a successful author, convinced me to share my story with the general public. I am grateful for the excellent reviews that I have received. I am not a professional writer, but I think that I have accomplished what I hoped the reader would find interesting. My intention is to be an inspiration to young people. I hope that the reader feels that we were sitting at a table having a conversation and that we live in a country that, with goals, hard work, and integrity, the average person can accomplish things beyond their wildest dreams. I am posting two excerpts from my previous book, and if anyone is interested in buying a signed copy, it can be purchased at larryreidy.net. No sales tax unless you are an Indiana resident.

Two excerpts from *My Quest for Life, Liberty, and the Pursuit of Happiness 1939–2019*:

> During one of my prospective dealer interviews for Sun Oil Company, I met a Shell dealer, Joe Lah, who told me he would give up his lease on the Queensgate station because it pumped too much gas. That seems counterintuitive, but Joe preferred to concentrate on service work as opposed to pumping gas. He was in the process of building a new station in a location where he felt the volume would be more in line with his preferences.
>
> Joe's station was not my first choice. My friend, Jack Sebastian, had been toying with retiring from his Shell station at Glenway Avenue and Werk Road in Western Hills. I preferred the Western Hills location, but at the last minute, Jack decided against retiring, so I took what was available.

I knew that going into business was not going to be easy because we had a savings account of five hundred dollars.

I negotiated a deal with Shell Oil Company to borrow money for my first gas tanker load of ten thousand gallons. It was to be paid back at one cent for every gallon of gas pumped through our new station.

I repaid the loan in four months.

I needed a loan from the bank for inventory and operating capital. Fortunately, I had previously helped several dealers obtaining loans through Central Trust Bank.

J.D. Alexander was a senior loan officer who later became president of Central Trust. Jim and I had a great relationship because of the dealer business I had generated for the bank.

I met with Jim and brought my business plan to show him that I was minimal risk for a five-thousand-dollar loan. Jim told me that he did not want to see my business plan. All he was interested in was my projected earnings and how long it would take me to pay back the loan.

I told Jim I would repay the loan within a year, and I expected to make thirty-six thousand dollars. He laughed and replied that he would go to work for me if I made that kind of money.

I told him no thanks, but he could buy me a steak dinner if I were proved right. I paid off the loan in seven months and made thirty-nine thousand dollars my first year in business.

The average income in 1965 was $6,900.00 per year.

Ralph and I shared quite a few experiences, but one shook him up. During the Cuban missile crisis, some ships were at sea for several months without shore leave.

When the sailors had liberty, we were instructed that they were supposed to be back on their ship by 1:00 A.M., but if they returned by 2:00, it was okay.

Ralph and I were on town patrol, and at about 12:45, we stopped in the nightclubs and told the sailors that the last call for a drink was 1:00.

We had one big problem at the Copacabana. There were eight or ten drunk sailors, with one exception. There was an Indian who was bigger than Bob Weeden, and he was drunk!

When I told them that it was the last call, the Neanderthal said that he wanted to see me make him leave. I told him to relax and enjoy his drink, and we would be back in about fifteen minutes.

He told me that he would be waiting for me. As we stopped in the other nightclubs, Ralph became increasingly nervous and said we should get some reinforcements. I told him, "don't worry; we got this." He asked if I was crazy or if I just wanted Tonto to kick both of our asses. I already had a plan, but I couldn't resist messing with Ralph, so I said if things start going bad, just shoot him.

He told me that I had mental problems, and we both started laughing. We stepped into the Copacabana, and the big guy had this I-am-drunk-out-of-my-mind smile waiting to put us both in the hospital.

Most of the sailors were probably nineteen to twenty-five years old, with one exception. He looked to be in his mid-thirties, so I walked over to him and said, "Chief, how long have you been in the Navy?" He told me that he was approaching fifteen years. I then informed him that if he didn't get that drunk asshole and the rest of his crew in cabs, Ralph would arrest him for inciting a riot and the rest of the drunks for public intoxication.

I informed him that they would all spend the rest of the weekend in a Panamanian jail while their ship went out to sea. He didn't reply, but he got everyone in cabs and they called us every lousy name they could think of as they hustled out the door.

About the Author

Larry Reidy is eighty-two years old and has been married to his wife, Nancy, for fifty-eight years. They have seven children, eighteen grandchildren, and five great-grandchildren. He served in the U.S. Army for three years active and three years in the National Guard. He is a retired small business owner after fifty-four years.

Forty-four years ago, they built their home in Batesville, Indiana. They love their community and the feel of small-town living. He thanks God for his longevity and hopes that he will have several years left to enjoy this great game of life. The challenge is, every day, trying to keep the old man out.